SECOND EDITION

Building Android Apps with HTML, CSS, and JavaScript

Jonathan Stark

with Brian Jepson

O'REILLY®

Beijing · Cambridge · Farnham · Köln · Sebastopol · Tokyo

Building Android Apps with HTML, CSS, and JavaScript, Second Edition
by Jonathan Stark with Brian Jepson

Published by O'Reilly Media, Inc., 1005 Gravenstein Highway North, Sebastopol, CA 95472.

O'Reilly books may be purchased for educational, business, or sales promotional use. Online editions are also available for most titles (*http://my.safaribooksonline.com*). For more information, contact our corporate/institutional sales department: (800) 998-9938 or *corporate@oreilly.com*.

Editor: Brian Jepson	**Cover Designer:** Karen Montgomery
Production Editor: Kristen Borg	**Interior Designer:** David Futato
Proofreader: O'Reilly Production Services	**Illustrator:** Robert Romano

September 2010: First Edition.
January 2012: Second Edition.

Revision History for the Second Edition:
  2012-01-10 First release
See *http://oreilly.com/catalog/errata.csp?isbn=9781449316419* for release details.

ISBN: 978-1-449-31641-9

[LSI]

1326207325

To Erica & Cooper

Table of Contents

Preface

Thanks to mobile phones, we have moved from virtually no one having access to information to virtually everyone having access to the vast resources of the Web. This is arguably the most important achievement of our generation. Despite its overarching importance, mobile computing is in its infancy. Technical, financial, and political forces have created platform fragmentation like never before, and it's going to get worse before it gets better.

Developers who need to engage large and diverse groups of people are faced with a seemingly impossible challenge: "How do we implement our mobile vision in a way that is feasible, affordable, and reaches the greatest number of participants?" In many cases, the answer is web technologies. The combination of advances in HTML5 and mobile devices has created an environment in which even novice developers can build mobile apps that improve people's lives on a global scale.

Google's Android operating system is a compelling addition to the mobile computing space. In true Google fashion, the platform is open, free, and highly interoperable. The development tools are full-featured and powerful, if a bit geeky, and run on a variety of platforms.

Carriers and handset manufacturers have jumped on the Android bandwagon. The market is beginning to flood with Android devices of all shapes and sizes. This is a double-edged sword for developers. On one hand, more devices mean a bigger market. On the other hand, more devices mean more fragmentation. As with the fragmentation in the general mobile market, fragmentation on Android can often be addressed by building apps with HTML, CSS, and JavaScript.

I'm the first to admit that not all apps are a good fit for development with web technologies. That said, I see a lot of apps written with native code that could have just as easily been done with HTML. When speaking to developers who aren't sure which approach to take, I say this:

If you can build your app with HTML, CSS, and JavaScript, you probably should.

Using open source, standards-based web technologies gives you the greatest flexibility, the broadest reach, and the lowest cost. You can easily release it as a web app, then debug and test it under load with thousands of real users. Once you are ready to rock, you can use PhoneGap to convert your web app to a native Android app, add a few device-specific features if you like, and submit to the Android Market or offer it for download from your website. Sounds good, right?

Who Should Read This Book

I'm going to assume you have some basic experience reading and writing HTML, CSS, and JavaScript (jQuery in particular). Chapter 5 includes some basic SQL code, so a passing familiarity with SQL syntax would be helpful but is not required.

What You Need to Use This Book

This book avoids the Android SDK wherever possible. All you need to follow along with the vast majority of examples is a text editor and the most recent version of Google Chrome (a cutting-edge web browser that's available for both Mac and Windows at *http://www.google.com/chrome*). You do need to have the Android SDK for the Phone-Gap material in Chapter 7, where I explain how to convert your web app into a native app that you can submit to the Android Market.

Conventions Used in This Book

The following typographical conventions are used in this book:

Italic
> Indicates new terms, URLs, email addresses, filenames, and file extensions.

`Constant width`
> Used for program listings, as well as within paragraphs to refer to program elements such as variable or function names, databases, data types, environment variables, statements, and keywords.

`Constant width bold`
> Shows commands or other text that should be typed literally by the user.

`Constant width italic`
> Shows text that should be replaced with user-supplied values or by values determined by context.

 This icon signifies a tip, suggestion, or general note.

This icon indicates a warning or caution.

Using Code Examples

This book is here to help you get your job done. In general, you may use the code in this book in your programs and documentation. You do not need to contact us for permission unless you're reproducing a significant portion of the code. For example, writing a program that uses several chunks of code from this book does not require permission. Selling or distributing a CD-ROM of examples from O'Reilly books does require permission. Answering a question by citing this book and quoting example code does not require permission. Incorporating a significant amount of example code from this book into your product's documentation does require permission.

We appreciate, but do not require, attribution. An attribution usually includes the title, author, publisher, and ISBN. For example: "*Building Android Apps with HTML, CSS, and JavaScript, 2nd edition* by Jonathan Stark (O'Reilly). Copyright 2012 Jonathan Stark, 978-1-4493-1641-9."

If you feel your use of code examples falls outside fair use or the permission given above, feel free to contact us at *permissions@oreilly.com*.

Safari® Books Online

 Safari Books Online is an on-demand digital library that lets you easily search over 7,500 technology and creative reference books and videos to find the answers you need quickly.

With a subscription, you can read any page and watch any video from our library online. Read books on your cell phone and mobile devices. Access new titles before they are available for print, and get exclusive access to manuscripts in development and post feedback for the authors. Copy and paste code samples, organize your favorites, download chapters, bookmark key sections, create notes, print out pages, and benefit from tons of other time-saving features.

O'Reilly Media has uploaded this book to the Safari Books Online service. To have full digital access to this book and others on similar topics from O'Reilly and other publishers, sign up for free at *http://my.safaribooksonline.com*.

How to Contact Us

Please address comments and questions concerning this book to the publisher:

O'Reilly Media, Inc.
1005 Gravenstein Highway North
Sebastopol, CA 95472
800-998-9938 (in the United States or Canada)
707-829-0515 (international or local)
707-829-0104 (fax)

We have a web page for this book, where we list errata, examples, and any additional information. You can access this page at:

http://shop.oreilly.com/product/0636920022886.do

To comment or ask technical questions about this book, send email to:

bookquestions@oreilly.com

For more information about our books, conferences, Resource Centers, and the O'Reilly Network, see our website at:

http://www.oreilly.com

Acknowledgments

Writing a book is a team effort. My heartfelt thanks go out to the following people for their generous contributions.

Tim O'Reilly, Brian Jepson, and the rest of the gang at ORM for making the experience of writing this book so rewarding and educational.

David Kaneda for his wonderfully obsessive pursuit of beauty. Whether it's a bit of code or a user interface animation, he can't sleep until it's perfect, and I love that.

The gang at Nitobi for creating and continuing to support PhoneGap.

Brian Fling for broadening my view of mobile beyond just the latest and greatest hardware. Brian knows mobile from back in the day; he's a wonderful writer, and on top of that, a very generous guy.

PPK, John Gruber, John Allsopp, and John Resig for their contributions to and support of the underlying technologies that made this book possible.

Joe Bowser, Brian LeRoux, Sara Czyzewicz, and the swarm of folks who generously posted comments and questions on the OFPS site for this book. Your feedback was very helpful and much appreciated.

My wonderful family, friends, and clients for being understanding and supportive while I was chained to the keyboard.

And finally, Erica. You make everything possible. I love you!

CHAPTER 1

Getting Started

Before we dive in, I'd like to quickly establish the playing field. In this chapter, I'll define key terms, compare the pros and cons of the two most common development approaches, and give a crash course on the three core web technologies used in this book.

Web Apps Versus Native Apps

First, I'd like to define what I mean by *web app* and *native app* and consider their pros and cons.

What Is a Web App?

To me, a web app is basically a website that is specifically optimized for use on a smartphone. The site content can be anything from a standard small business brochure site to a mortgage calculator to a daily calorie tracker—the content is irrelevant. The defining characteristics of a web app are that the user interface (UI) is built with web standard technologies, it is available at a URL (public, private, or perhaps behind a login), and it is optimized for the characteristics of a mobile device. A web app is not installed on the phone, it is not available in the Android Market, and it is not written with Java.

What Is a Native App?

In contrast, native apps are installed on the Android phone, they have access to the hardware (speakers, accelerometer, camera, etc.), and they are written with Java. The defining characteristic of a native app, however, is that it's available in the Android Market—a feature that has captured the imagination of a horde of software entrepreneurs worldwide, myself included.

Pros and Cons

Different applications have different requirements. Some apps are a better fit with web technologies than others. Knowing the pros and cons of each approach will help you make a better decision about which path is appropriate for your situation.

Here are the pros of native app development:

- Millions of registered credit card owners are one click away
- You can access all the cool hardware features of the device

Here are the cons of native app development:

- You have to pay to become an Android developer
- Your app will run only on Android phones
- You have to develop using Java
- The development cycle is slow (develop, compile, deploy, repeat)

Here are the pros of web app development:

- Web developers can use their current authoring tools
- You can use your current web design and development skills
- Your app will run on any device that has a web browser
- You can fix bugs in real time
- The development cycle is fast

Here are the cons of web app development:

- You cannot access the all cool hardware features of the phone
- You have to roll your own payment system if you want to charge for the app
- It can be difficult to achieve sophisticated UI effects

Which Approach Is Right for You?

Here's where it gets exciting. The always-online nature of the Android phone creates an environment in which the lines between a web app and a native app get blurry. There are even some little-known features of the Android web browser (see Chapter 6) that allow you to take a web app offline if you want. What's more, several third-party projects—of which PhoneGap is the most notable—are actively developing solutions that allow web developers to take a web app and package it as a native app for Android and other mobile platforms.

For me, this is the perfect blend. I can write in my preferred language, release a product as a pure web app (for Android and any other devices that have a modern browser), and use the same code base to create an enhanced native version that can access the device hardware and potentially be sold in the Android Market. This is a great way to create a "freemium" model for your app—allow free access to the web app and charge for the more feature-rich native version.

Web Programming Crash Course

The three main technologies we will use to build web apps are HTML, CSS, and JavaScript. We'll quickly cover each to make sure we're all on the same page before plowing into the fancy stuff.

Introduction to HTML

When you are browsing the web, the pages you are viewing are just text documents sitting on someone else's computer. The text in a typical web page is wrapped in HTML tags, which tell your browser about the structure of the document. With this information, the browser can decide how to display the information in a way that makes sense.

Consider the web page snippet shown in Example 1-1. On the first line, the string Hi there! is wrapped in a pair of h1 tags. Notice that the *open tag* and the *close tag* are slightly different: the close tag has a slash (/) as the second character, while the open tag does not have a slash.

Wrapping text in h1 tags tells the browser that the words enclosed are a heading, which will cause it to be displayed in large bold text on its own line. There are also h2, h3, h4, h5, and h6 heading tags. The lower the number, the more important the header, so text wrapped in an h6 tag will be smaller (i.e., less important-looking) than text wrapped in an h3 tag.

After the h1 tag in Example 1-1, there are two lines wrapped in p tags. These are called paragraph tags. Browsers will display each paragraph on its own line. If the paragraph is long enough to exceed the width of the browser window, the text will bump down and continue on the next line. In either case, a blank line will be inserted after the paragraph to separate it from the next item on the page.

Example 1-1. HTML snippet

```
<h1>Hi there!</h1>
<p>Thanks for visiting my web page.</p>
<p>I hope you like it.</p>
```

You can also put HTML tags inside other HTML tags. Example 1-2 shows an unordered list (ul) tag that contains three list items (li). In a browser, this appears as a bulleted list with each item on its own line. When you have a tag or tags inside another tag, the inner tags are called *child elements*, or children, of the parent tag. So in this example, the li tags are children of the ul parent.

Example 1-2. Unordered list

```
<ul>
    <li>Pizza</li>
    <li>Beer</li>
    <li>Dogs</li>
</ul>
```

The tags covered so far are all *block tags*. The defining characteristic of block tags is that they are displayed on a line of their own, with no elements to the left or right of them. That is why the heading, paragraphs, and list items progress down the page instead of across it. The opposite of a block tag is an *inline tag*, which, as the name implies, can appear in a line. The emphasis tag (em) is an example of an inline tag, and it looks like this:

```
<p>I <em>really</em> hope you like it.</p>
```

The granddaddy of the inline tags—and arguably the coolest feature of HTML—is the a tag. The "a" stands for anchor, but at times I'll also refer to it as a link or hyperlink. Text wrapped in an anchor tag is clickable, such that clicking on it causes the browser to load a new HTML page.

To tell the browser which new page to load, we have to add what's called an *attribute* to the tag. Attributes are named values that you insert into an open tag. In an anchor tag, you use the href attribute to specify the location of the target page. Here's a link to Google's home page:

```
<a href="http://www.google.com/">Google</a>
```

That might look like a bit of a jumble if you are not used to reading HTML, but you should be able to pick out the URL for the Google home page. You'll be seeing a lot of a tags and href attributes throughout the book, so take a minute to get your head around this if it doesn't make sense at first glance.

 There are a couple of things to keep in mind regarding attributes. Different HTML tags allow different attributes. You can add multiple attributes to an open tag by separating them with spaces. You never add attributes to a closing tag. There are hundreds of possible combinations of attributes and tags, but don't sweat it—we only have to worry about a dozen or so in this entire book.

The HTML snippet that we've been looking at would normally reside in the body section of a complete HTML document. An HTML document is made up of two sections: the head and the body. The body is where you put all the content that you want users to see. The head contains information about the page, most of which is invisible to the user.

The body and head are always wrapped in an `html` element. Example 1-3 shows the snippet in the context of a proper HTML document. For now the `head` section contains a `title` element, which tells the browser what text to display in the title bar of the window.

Example 1-3. A proper HTML document

```html
<html>
    <head>
        <title>My Awesome Page</title>
    </head>
    <body>
        <h1>Hi there!</h1>
        <p>Thanks for visiting my web page.</p>
        <p>I hope you like it.</p>
        <ul>
            <li>Pizza</li>
            <li>Beer</li>
            <li>Dogs</li>
        </ul>
    </body>
</html>
```

Normally, when you are using your web browser you are viewing pages that are hosted on the Internet. However, browsers are perfectly good at displaying HTML documents that are on your local machine as well. To show you what I mean, I invite you to crack open a text editor and enter the code in Example 1-3.

Picking the Right Text Editor

Some text editors are not suited for authoring HTML. In particular, you want to avoid editors that support rich text editing, like Microsoft WordPad (Windows) or TextEdit (Mac OS X). These types of editors can save their files in formats other than plain text, which will break your HTML. If you must use TextEdit, save in plain text by choosing Format→Make Plain Text. In Windows, use Notepad instead of WordPad.

If you are in the market for a good text editor, my recommendation on the Mac is TextMate (*http://macromates.com/*). For Windows, both the E Text Editor (*http://www.e-texteditor.com/*) and Sublime Text (*http://www.sublimetext.com/*) are great.

If free is your thing, you can download Text Wrangler (*http://www.barebones.com/products/TextWrangler/*) for Mac. For Windows, Notepad2 (*http://www.flos-freeware.ch/notepad2.html*) and Notepad++ (*http://notepad-plus-plus.org/*) are highly regarded. Linux comes with an assortment of text editors, such as vi, nano, emacs, and gedit.

When you are finished entering the code from Example 1-3, save it to your desktop as *test.html* and then open it with Chrome by either dragging the file onto the Chrome application icon or opening Chrome and selecting File→Open File. Double-clicking *test.html* will work as well, but it could open in your text editor or another browser, depending on your settings.

Even if it's not your favorite browser, you should use Chrome when testing your Android web apps on a desktop web browser, because Chrome is the closest desktop browser to Android's mobile browser. Chrome is available for Mac and Windows from *http://google.com/ chrome*.

Introduction to CSS

As you've seen, browsers render certain HTML elements with distinct styles (for example, headings are large and bold, paragraphs are followed by a blank line, and so forth). These styles are very basic and are primarily intended to help the reader understand the structure and meaning of the document.

To go beyond this simple structure-based rendering, you use Cascading Style Sheets (CSS). CSS is a stylesheet language that you use to define the visual presentation of an HTML document. You can use CSS to define simple things like the text color, size, and style (bold, italic, etc.), or complex things like page layout, gradients, opacity, and much more.

Example 1-4 shows a CSS rule that instructs the browser to display any text in the body element using the color red. In this example, body is the *selector* (this specifies what is affected by the rule) and the curly braces enclose the *declaration* (the rule itself). The declaration includes a set of *properties* and their *values*. In this example, color is the property, and red is the value of the color property.

Example 1-4. A simple CSS rule

```
body { color: red; }
```

Property names are predefined in the CSS specification, which means that you can't just make them up. Each property expects an appropriate value, and there can be lots of appropriate values and value formats for a given property.

For example, you can specify colors with predefined keywords like red, or by using HTML color code notation, which uses a hexadecimal notation: a hash/pound sign (#) followed by three pairs of hexadecimal digits (0–F) representing (from left to right) red, green, and blue values (red is represented as #FF0000). Properties that expect measurements can accept values like 10px, 75%, and 1em. Example 1-5 shows some common declarations. The color code shown for background-color corresponds to the CSS "gray."

Example 1-5. Some common CSS declarations

```
body {
    color: red;
    background-color: #808080;
    font-size: 12px;
    font-style: italic;
```

```
    font-weight: bold;
    font-family: Arial;
}
```

Selectors come in a variety of flavors. If you want all of your hyperlinks (the a element) to display in italics, add the following to your stylesheet:

```
a { font-style: italic; }
```

If you want to be more specific and only italicize the hyperlinks that are contained somewhere within an h1 tag, add the following to your stylesheet:

```
h1 a { font-style: italic; }
```

You can also define your own custom selectors by adding id and/or class attributes to your HTML tags. Consider the following HTML snippet:

```
<h1 class="loud">Hi there!</h1>
<p id="highlight"> Thanks for visiting my web page.</p>
<p>I hope you like it.</p>
<ul>
    <li class="loud">Pizza</li>
    <li>Beer</li>
    <li>Dogs</li>
</ul>
```

If we add (more on this in a moment) .loud { font-style: italic; } to the CSS for this HTML, Hi there! and Pizza will show up italicized because they both have the loud class. The dot in front of the .loud selector is important—it's how the CSS knows to look for HTML tags with a class of loud. If you omit the dot, the CSS will look for a loud tag, which doesn't exist in this snippet (or in HTML at all, for that matter).

Applying CSS by id is similar. To add a yellow background fill to the highlight paragraph tag, use the following rule:

```
#highlight { background-color: yellow; }
```

Here, the # symbol tells the CSS to look for an HTML tag with the ID highlight.

To recap, you can opt to select elements by tag name (e.g., body, h1, p), by class name (e.g., .loud, .subtle, .error), or by ID (e.g., #highlight, #login, #promo). And, you can get more specific by chaining selectors together (e.g., h1 a, body ul .loud).

There are differences between class and id. Use class attributes when you have more than one item on the page with the same class value. Conversely, id values have to be unique to a page.

When I first learned this, I figured I'd just always use class attributes so I wouldn't have to worry about whether I was duping an ID value. However, selecting elements by ID is much faster than by class, so you can hurt your performance by overusing class selectors.

Applying a stylesheet

So now you understand the basics of CSS, but how do you apply a stylesheet to an HTML page? Quite simple, actually! First, you save the CSS somewhere on your server (usually in the same directory as your HTML file, though you can put it in a subdirectory). Next, link to the stylesheet in the head of the HTML document, as shown in Example 1-6. The href attribute in this example is a relative path, meaning it points to a text file named *screen.css* in the same directory as the HTML page. You can also specify absolute links, such as the following:

> *http://example.com/screen.css*

 If you are saving your HTML files on your local machine, you'll want to keep things simple: put the CSS file in the same directory as the HTML file and use a relative path, as shown in Example 1-6.

Example 1-6. Linking to a CSS stylesheet

```html
<html>
    <head>
        <title>My Awesome Page</title>
        <link rel="stylesheet" href="screen.css" type="text/css" />
    </head>
    <body>
        <h1 class="loud">Hi there!</h1>
        <p id="highlight"> Thanks for visiting my web page.</p>
        <p>I hope you like it.</p>
        <ul>
            <li class="loud">Pizza</li>
            <li>Beer</li>
            <li>Dogs</li>
        </ul>
    </body>
</html>
```

Example 1-7 shows the contents of *screen.css*. You should save this file in the same location as the HTML file.

Example 1-7. A simple stylesheet

```css
body {
    font-size: 12px;
    font-weight: bold;
    font-family: Arial;
}

a { font-style: italic; }
h1 a { font-style: italic; }

.loud { font-style: italic; }
#highlight { background-color: yellow; }
```

It's worth pointing out that you can link to stylesheets that are hosted on domains other than the one hosting the HTML document. However, it's considered very rude to link to someone else's stylesheets without permission, so please only link to your own.

For a quick and thorough crash course in CSS, I highly recommend *CSS Pocket Reference: Visual Presentation for the Web* by Eric Meyer (O'Reilly). Meyer is the last word when it comes to CSS, and this particular book is short enough to read during the typical morning carpool (unless you are the person driving, in which case it could take considerably longer—did I say "crash" course?).

Introduction to JavaScript

At this point you know how to structure a document with HTML and how to modify its visual presentation with CSS. Now I'll show you how JavaScript can make the web do stuff.

JavaScript is a scripting language that you can add to an HTML page to make it more interactive and convenient for the user. For example, you can write some JavaScript that will inspect the values typed in a form to make sure they are valid. Or, you can have JavaScript show or hide elements of a page depending on where the user clicks. JavaScript can even contact the web server to execute database changes without refreshing the current web page.

Like any modern scripting language, JavaScript has variables, arrays, objects, and all the typical control structures (e.g., `if`, `while`, `for`). Example 1-8 shows a snippet of JavaScript that illustrates many core concepts of the language (don't try putting this in your HTML file yet; I'll show you how to combine HTML and JavaScript in a moment).

Example 1-8. Basic JavaScript syntax

```
var foods = ['Apples', 'Bananas', 'Oranges']; ❶
for (var i=0; i<foods.length; i++) { ❷
  if (foods[i] == 'Apples') { ❸
    alert(foods[i] + ' are my favorite!'); ❹
  } else {
    alert(foods[i] + ' are okay.'); ❺
  }
}
```

Here's an explanation of what's happening here:

❶ Define an *array* (a list of values) named `foods` that contains three elements.

❷ Open a typical `for` loop that initializes a variable named `i` to 0 and specifies an exit criteria—in this case, exit when `i` is greater than the length of the `foods` array, and increment `i` by 1 each time through the loop (`i++` is shorthand for "add 1 to the current value of `i`").

❸ A garden variety `if` that checks to see if the current element of the array is equal to Apples.

❹ Displayed if the current element of the array is equal to Apples.

❺ Displayed if the current element of the array is *not* equal to Apples.

Here are some points about JavaScript's syntax that are worth noting:

- Statements are terminated with semicolons (;)
- Code blocks are enclosed in curly braces ({})
- Variables are declared using the **var** keyword
- Array elements can be accessed with square bracket notation ([])
- Array keys are assigned beginning at 0
- The single equals sign (=) is the assignment operator (assigns a value to a variable)
- The double equals sign (==) is the equivalence logical operator (compares two values and evaluates to true if they are equivalent)
- The plus sign (+) is the string concatenation operator (combines two strings together)

For our purposes, the most important feature of JavaScript is that it can interact with the elements of an HTML page (the cool kids call this "manipulating the DOM"). Example 1-9 shows a simple bit of JavaScript that changes some text on the page when the user clicks on the **h1**. Create a new file in your text editor, save it as *onclick.html*, and open the document in your browser. Click the text labeled "Click me!" and watch it change.

 DOM stands for Document Object Model and in this context it represents the browser's understanding of an HTML page. You can read more about the DOM here: *http://en.wikipedia.org/wiki/Document_Object _Model*.

Example 1-9. Simple onclick handler

```html
<html>
    <head>
        <title>My Awesome Page</title>
        <script type="text/javascript" charset="utf-8"> ❶
            function sayHello() { ❷
                document.getElementById('foo').innerHTML = 'Hi there!'; ❸
            } ❹
        </script> ❺
    </head>
    <body>
        <h1 id="foo" onclick="sayHello()">Click me!</h1>❻
    </body>
</html>
```

Here's an explanation:

❶ A script block at the head of the HTML document.

❷ This line defines a single JavaScript function named `sayHello()` inside the script block.

❸ The `sayHello()` function contains a single statement that tells the browser to look through the document for an element that has the ID `foo`, and set its inner HTML contents to `Hi there!` The effect of this in the browser is that the text "Click me!" will be replaced with "Hi there!" when the user clicks the `h1` element.

❹ End of the `sayHello()` function.

❺ End of the script block.

❻ The `onclick` attribute of the `h1` element tells the browser to do something when the user clicks the `h1` element, namely, to run the `sayHello()` function.

Back in the bad old days of web development, different browsers had different support for JavaScript. This meant that your code might run in Safari 2 but not in Internet Explorer 6. You had to take great pains to test each browser (and even different versions of the same browser) to make sure your code would work for everyone. As the number of browsers and browser versions grew, it became impossible to test and maintain your JavaScript code for every environment. At that time, web programming with JavaScript was hell.

Enter jQuery. jQuery is a relatively small JavaScript library that allows you to write your JavaScript code in a way that will work the same in a wide variety of browsers. What's more, it greatly simplifies a number of common web development tasks. For these reasons, I use jQuery in most of my web development work, and I'll be using it for the JavaScript examples in this book. Example 1-10 is a jQuery rewrite of Example 1-9. Create a new file in your text editor, copy this listing into it, and save it as *jquerytest.html*. Next, download *jquery.js* into the same directory. Then open the file in your web browser and try it out.

 jQuery downloads, documentation, and tutorials are available at *http: //jquery.com*. To use jQuery as shown in Example 1-9, you will need to download it from there, rename the file you downloaded (such as *jquery-1.4.2.min.js*) to *jquery.js*, and put a copy of it in the same directory as your HTML document.

Example 1-10. jQuery onclick handler

```
<html>
    <head>
        <title>My Awesome Page</title>
        <script type="text/javascript" src="jquery.js"></script> ❶
        <script type="text/javascript" charset="utf-8">
```

```
        function sayHello() {
            $('#foo').text('Hi there!'); ❷
        }
    </script>
  </head>
  <body>
    <h1 id="foo" onclick="sayHello()">Click me!</h1>
  </body>
</html>
```

❶ This line includes the *jquery.js* library. It uses a relative path, meaning the file exists in the same directory as the page that is using it (this example won't function correctly unless the jQuery library, *jquery.js*, is there). However, you can include it directly from a variety of places where it's available.

❷ Notice the reduction in the amount of code we need to write to replace the text in the h1 element. This might not seem like a big deal in such a trivial example, but I can assure you that it's a lifesaver in complex solutions.

We'll be seeing plenty of real-world jQuery examples later on, so I'm going to leave it at that for the moment.

CHAPTER 2

Basic Styling

Ultimately, we are going to build a native Android app using HTML, CSS, and Java-Script. The first step on this journey is to get comfortable styling HTML to look like a mobile app. In this chapter, I'll show you how to apply CSS styles to a bunch of existing HTML pages so that they are easily navigable on an Android phone. So, in addition to moving closer to building a native app, you'll be learning a practical (and valuable) skill that you can use immediately.

Don't Have a Website?

If you've been testing all your web pages locally on your personal computer, you won't be able to view them on your Android phone without setting up a server. You have a couple choices:

- Host your web pages on a web server and connect to that server from your Android phone. Chances are good that your Internet Service Provider (ISP) offers complimentary web hosting, but this usually only supports basic features such as HTML. By the time we get to Chapter 6, we're going to need to use PHP, a scripting language that runs on the web server, so you should look into an inexpensive hosting service. Many companies, such as Laughing Squid (*http://laughingsquid.us/*), offer entry-level hosting with PHP for under $10 a month.

- Host them on a web server running on your computer and connect to the web server running on your computer from your Android phone. This only works when your Android phone and computer are on the same WiFi network.

This chapter is set up so you can try the examples as you go through it. So, no matter which option you choose for viewing the web pages, try reloading them in a browser (preferably the Android browser) each time you add something new to one of the samples. However, be sure to save your file in your text editor before you reload it in the browser, or you won't see your changes.

Running a Web Server Locally

Linux, Windows, and Mac OS X each include some sort of web server. On Mac OS X, open System Preferences, choose Sharing, and enable Web Sharing. Once you've started Web Sharing, the Web Sharing preferences will display the URL of your personal website (this includes anything you've put in the *Sites* directory in your home directory). It will be of the form `http://local-hostname/~your-username`. After you start Web Sharing, try putting the *test.html* file you created in Chapter 1 into the *Sites* directory in your home directory. Click the link shown in the Web Sharing preferences pane (which might be something like *http://10.0.1.29/~your-username/*), and then add `test.html` after the URL (leaving you with something like *http://10.0.1.29/~your-user name/test.html*), and load that page.

On Windows, open the Control Panel, choose Programs, and click Turn Windows Features On or Off. Check the box labeled Internet Information Services and then click the + to its left; continue to drill down into World Wide Web Services→Application Development Features, then check the box to enable CGI (you'll need the CGI feature to install PHP in Chapter 6). Click OK. After you've done this, you can put your web documents in your IIS document root, which is typically located at *C:\inetpub \wwwroot*. Try this with the *test.html* file you created in Chapter 1; you should be able to load that file by going to *http://localhost/test.html* in your browser.

You'll probably need to authenticate each time you put files into that folder. To work around this problem, you can either use the IIS Manager (Start→Control Panel→System and Security→Administrative Tools) to add a new virtual directory in a folder you have permissions to modify, or you can give yourself control of *C:\inetpub\wwwroot* (right-click on the folder, choose Properties→Security, and then click Edit→Add, type your username, click OK, then allow Full Control and click OK). If you want to connect to your Windows web server, even over your local network, you'll need to go into the Control Panel→System and Security→Windows Firewall→Allow A Program or Feature Through Windows Firewall and enable World Wide Web Services.

If you'd prefer to run Apache on Windows, check out a prepackaged solution such as EasyPHP (*http://www.easyphp.org/*), or check out the Wikipedia page on this topic at *http://en.wikipedia.org/wiki/Comparison_of_WAMPs*.

On some versions of Linux, such as Ubuntu, you will need to go through some additional steps to install and enable a web server. For example, on Ubuntu, you can install Apache at the command line with `sudo apt-get install apache2`. Next, enable the user directory module with `sudo a2enmod userdir`. Once that's done, restart Apache with this command: `sudo /etc/init.d/apache2 restart`. After you've done that, you can create a directory called *public_html* in your home directory and access any files in there with a URL such as `http://local-hostname/~your-username`.

First Steps

Theory is great, but I'm a "show me, don't tell me" kinda guy, so let's dive in.

Imagine you have a website that you want to "mobile-ize" (Figure 2-1). In this scenario, there are a number of easy things you can do to optimize a site for Android. I'll go over your options in this chapter. Example 2-1 shows an abbreviated version of the website shown in Figure 2-2. This is the HTML you'll be working with in this chapter.

Figure 2-2 shows what the abbreviated version of the web page looks like on the Android phone, and Figure 2-3 shows it on the desktop version of Chrome for comparison. It's usable, but far from optimized for Android.

> If you'd like to try styling this example as you go through the chapter, you can download the HTML and supporting files from this book's website (see "How to Contact Us" on page xii). The desktop stylesheet (*screen.css*) is not shown as it is not essential, but you can use the stylesheet from the previous chapter if you'd like to have something to play with.

Figure 2-1. The desktop version of a typical website looks fine on a large screen

Example 2-1. The HTML document we'll be styling

```html
<html>
<head>
  <link rel="stylesheet" href="screen.css" type="text/css" />
  <title>Jonathan Stark</title>
</head>
<body>
<div id="container">
  <div id="header">
    <h1><a href="./">Jonathan Stark</a></h1>
    <div id="utility">
        <ul>
            <li><a href="about.html">About</a></li>
            <li><a href="blog.html">Blog</a></li>
            <li><a href="contact.html">Contact</a></li>
        </ul>
    </div>
    <div id="nav">
        <ul>
            <li><a href="consulting-clinic.html">Consulting Clinic</a></li>
            <li><a href="on-call.html">On Call</a></li>
            <li><a href="development.html">Development</a></li>
            <li><a href="http://www.oreilly.com">O'Reilly Media, Inc.</a></li>
        </ul>
    </div>
  </div>
  <div id="content">
    <h2>About</h2>
    <p>Jonathan Stark is a web developer, speaker, and author. His
        consulting firm, Jonathan Stark Consulting, Inc., has attracted
        clients such as Staples, Turner Broadcasting, and the PGA Tour.
        ...
        </p>
  </div>
  <div id="sidebar">
    <img alt="Manga Portrait of Jonathan Stark"
        src="jonathanstark-manga-small.png"/>
    <p>Jonathan Stark is a mobile and web application developer who the
        Wall Street Journal has called an expert on publishing desktop
        data to the web.</p>
  </div>
  <div id="footer">
    <ul>
        <li><a href="services.html">Services</a></li>
        <li><a href="about.html">About</a></li>
        <li><a href="blog.html">Blog</a></li>
    </ul>
    <p class="subtle">Jonathan Stark Consulting, Inc.</p>
  </div>
</div>
</body>
</html>
```

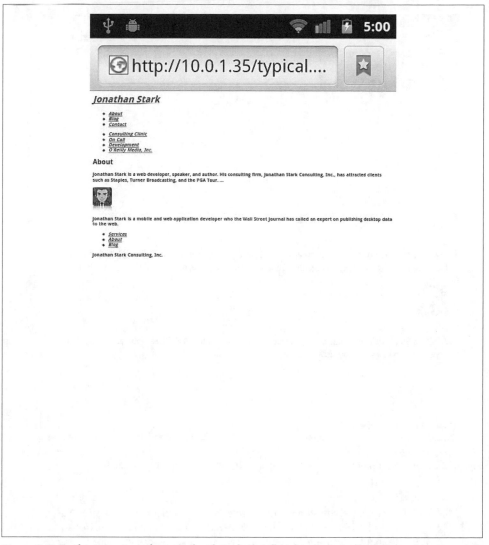

Figure 2-2. Desktop version of a typical website looks all right on an Android phone, but we can do a lot better

Figure 2-3. Desktop version of the abbreviated web page in the Chrome browser

For years, web developers used tables to lay out elements in a grid. Advances in CSS and HTML have rendered that approach not only obsolete, but undesirable. Today, we primarily use the `div` element (along with a variety of attributes) to accomplish the same thing, but with more control. Although a complete explanation of div-based layouts is well outside the scope of this book, you'll see plenty of examples of it as you read through the book. To learn more, please check out *Designing with Web Standards* by Jeffrey Zeldman (New Rider Press), which covers the issue in greater detail.

Prepare a Separate Android Stylesheet

I'm as DRY as the next guy but for the sake of clarity I'm going to make a clean break between our desktop browser stylesheet and the Android stylesheet. This approach goes against the concepts of Responsive Web Design, and may or may not make sense for your web site (or web app) depending on a variety of factors. An in depth discussion of Responsive Web Design is beyond the scope of this book, but if you're working in mobile, you should spend some time getting familiar with the concepts involved. The definitive article was posted by Ethan Marcotte on A List Apart (*http://www.alistapart .com/articles/responsive-web-design/*).

DRY stands for "don't repeat yourself," and is a software development principle that states, "Every piece of knowledge must have a single, un-ambiguous, authoritative representation within a system." The term was coined by Andrew Hunt and David Thomas in their book *The Pragmatic Programmer* (Addison-Wesley Professional).

To specify a stylesheet specifically for Android (as well as any similarly small device such as the iPhone or Windows Phone), replace the stylesheet link tag in the sample HTML document with ones that use the following expressions:

```
<link rel="stylesheet" type="text/css"
      href="android.css" media="only screen and (max-width: 600px)" />
<link rel="stylesheet" type="text/css"
      href="desktop.css" media="screen and (min-width: 601px)" />
```

I specifically used `max-width` and `min-width` here so that you can resize your desktop browser and see the mobile version of the page.

The Wireless Universal Resource File (WURFL) contains information you can use to identify a huge number of wireless devices, including Android devices. If you need to detect Android devices with a width greater than 600px (such as a tablet) or if you don't want the mobile version of the site to appear when users resize their browser window below 600px, you can use WURFL's PHP API to precisely detect specific browsers. See the Appendix for more information on WURFL.

Here, *desktop.css* refers to your existing desktop stylesheet, and *android.css* is a new file that we'll be discussing in detail in a bit. The *desktop.css* file is not essential, but you can use the stylesheet from the previous chapter if you'd like.

If you're following along using the sample HTML document shown in Example 2-1, you'll need to rename *screen.css* to *desktop.css*, but since we're focused on the Android stylesheet, you can ignore the desktop stylesheet completely. If it fails to load, your browser won't get too upset.

However, if you'd like to use Chrome to test the Android-optimized version of the site, you should replace the reference to *desktop.css* with a reference to *android.css*. That way, you'll get to run the Android version of your site whether you load it from a phone or the desktop browser.

Regrettably, Internet Explorer will not understand these expressions, so we have to add a conditional comment (shown in bold) that links to the desktop version of the CSS:

```
<link rel="stylesheet" type="text/css"
    href="android.css" media="only screen and (max-width: 600px)" />
<link rel="stylesheet" type="text/css"
    href="desktop.css" media="screen and (min-width: 601px)" />
<!--[if IE]>
<link rel="stylesheet" type="text/css" href="desktop.css" media="all" />
<![endif]-->
```

So now it's time to edit the HTML document (if you haven't already done that as you were following along)—delete the existing `link` to the *screen.css* file, and replace it with the lines just shown. This way, you will have a clean slate for the Android-specific CSS in this chapter.

Control the Page Scaling

Unless you tell it otherwise, the Android browser will assume your page is 980px wide (you can see this back in Figure 2-2). In the majority of cases, this works great. However, you are going to format the content specifically for the smaller dimensions of the Android phone, so you must let the mobile browser know about it by adding a viewport `meta` tag to the `head` element of the HTML document:

```
<meta name="viewport" content="user-scalable=no, width=device-width" />
```

Desktop browsers will ignore the viewport `meta` tag, so you can include it without worrying about the desktop version of your site.

Merely by suppressing the desktop stylesheet and configuring your viewport, you will have already given your Android users an enhanced experience (see Figure 2-4). To really impress them, let's start building the *android.css* stylesheet.

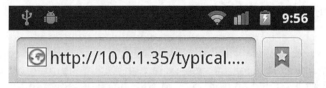

Jonathan Stark

- About
- Blog
- Contact

- Consulting Clinic
- On Call
- Development
- O'Reilly Media, Inc.

About

Jonathan Stark is a web developer, speaker, and author. His consulting firm, Jonathan Stark Consulting, Inc., has attracted clients such as Staples, Turner Broadcasting, and the PGA Tour. ...

Figure 2-4. Setting the viewport to the width of the device makes your pages a lot more readable on Android

 If you don't set the viewport width, the page will be zoomed out when it first loads. It's tough to say exactly what the zoom level will be because the Android browser includes a setting that allows users to set the default zoom. The options are Far, Medium (the default), or Close. Even if you do set the viewport width, these user-defined settings will affect the zoom level of your app.

Adding the Android CSS

There are a number of UI conventions that make an Android app look like an Android app. In the next section, we'll add the distinctive title bar, lists with rounded corners, finger-friendly links that look like glossy buttons, etc. With the text editor of your choice, create a file named *android.css* and add the code shown in Example 2-2 to it, then save the file in the same directory as your HTML document.

Example 2-2. Setting some general site-wide styles on the HTML body element

```
body {
    background-color: #ddd; /* Background color */
    color: #222;            /* Foreground color used for text */
    font-family: Helvetica;
    font-size: 14px;
    margin: 0;              /* Amount of negative space around the
                               outside of the body */
    padding: 0;             /* Amount of negative space around the
                               inside of the body */
}
```

 All text on Android is rendered using a custom font named Droid (as of Android 4.0, Droid has been replaced by a new font, Roboto). The Droid font family was specifically built for mobile devices, has excellent character set support, and contains three variants: Droid Sans, Droid Sans Mono, and Droid Serif. Therefore, specifying a font family of Helvetica as we've done here will only have an effect on devices other than Android.

Now let's attack the header **div** that contains the main home link (i.e., the logo link) and the primary and secondary site navigation. The first step is to format the logo link as a clickable title bar. Add the following to the *android.css* file:

```
#header h1 {
    margin: 0;
    padding: 0;
}
#header h1 a {
    background-color: #ccc;
    border-bottom: 1px solid #666;
    color: #222;
    display: block;
    font-size: 20px;
    font-weight: bold;
    padding: 10px 0;
    text-align: center;
    text-decoration: none;
}
```

We'll format the primary and secondary navigation ul blocks identically, so we can just use the generic tag selectors (i.e., #header ul) as opposed to the tag IDs (i.e., #header ul#utility, #header ul#nav):

```css
#header ul {
    list-style: none;
    margin: 10px;
    padding: 0;
}
#header ul li a {
    background-color: #FFFFFF;
    border: 1px solid #999999;
    color: #222222;
    display: block;
    font-size: 17px;
    font-weight: bold;
    margin-bottom: -1px;
    padding: 12px 10px;
    text-decoration: none;
}
```

Pretty simple so far, right? With this little bit of CSS, we have already made a big improvement on the Android page design (Figure 2-5). Next, add some padding to the content and sidebar divs to indent the text from the edge of the screen a bit (Figure 2-6):

```css
#content, #sidebar {
    padding: 10px;
}
```

 You might be wondering why we're adding padding to the content and sidebar elements instead of setting it globally on the body element itself. The reason is that it's very common to have elements displayed edge to edge (as with the header in this example). Because of this, padding applied to the body or some other element that's wrapped around lots of others can become more trouble than it's worth.

The content in the footer of this page is basically a rehash of the navigation element (the ul element with the ID nav) at the top of the page, so you can remove the footer from the Android version of the page by setting the display to none, as follows:

```css
#footer {
    display: none;
}
```

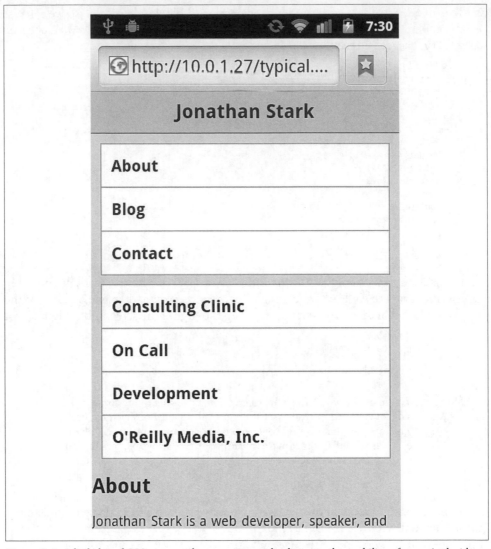

Figure 2-5. A little bit of CSS can go a long way toward enhancing the usability of your Android app

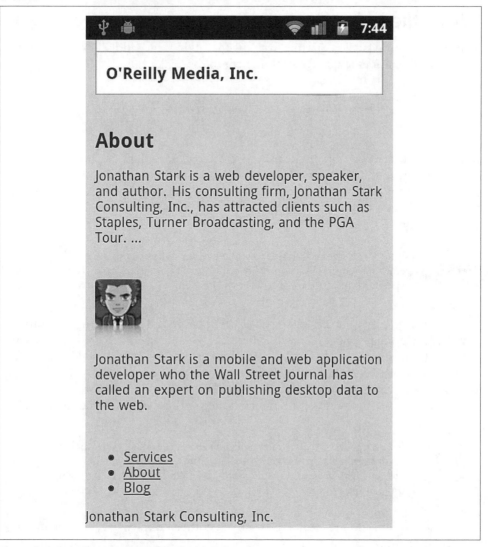

Figure 2-6. Indenting text from the edges

Adding the Android Look and Feel

Time to get a little fancier. Starting from the top of the page, add a 1-pixel white drop shadow to the header text and a CSS gradient to the background:

```
#header h1 a {
    text-shadow: 0px 1px 1px #fff;
    background-image: -webkit-gradient(linear, left top, left bottom,
                                    from(#ccc), to(#999));
}
```

In the `text-shadow` declaration, the parameters from left to right are: horizontal offset, vertical offset, blur, and color. Most of the time, you'll be applying the exact values shown here to your text because that's what usually looks good on Android, but it is fun to experiment with `text-shadow` because it can add a subtle but sophisticated touch to your design.

 On most browsers, it's fine to specify a blur radius of 0px. However, Android requires you to specify a blur radius of at least 1px. If you specify a blur of 0, the text shadow will not show up on Android devices.

The `-webkit-gradient` line deserves special attention. It's an instruction to the browser to generate a gradient image on the fly. Therefore, you can use a CSS gradient anywhere you would normally specify a `url()` (e.g., background image, list style image). The parameters from left to right are as follows: the gradient type (can be `linear` or `radial`), the starting point of the gradient (can be `left top`, `left bottom`, `right top`, or `right bottom`), the end point of the gradient, the starting color, and the ending color.

 You cannot reverse the horizontal and vertical portions of the four gradient start and stop point constants (i.e., `left top`, `left bottom`, `right top`, or `right bottom`). In other words, top left, bottom left, top right, and bottom right are invalid values.

The next step is to add the traditional rounded corners to the navigation menus:

```
#header ul li:first-child a {
    -webkit-border-top-left-radius: 8px;
    -webkit-border-top-right-radius: 8px;
}
#header ul li:last-child a {
    -webkit-border-bottom-left-radius: 8px;
    -webkit-border-bottom-right-radius: 8px;
}
```

As you can see, we're using corner-specific versions of the `-webkit-border-radius` property to apply an 8-pixel radius to both the top two corners of the first list item and the bottom two corners of the last list item (Figure 2-7).

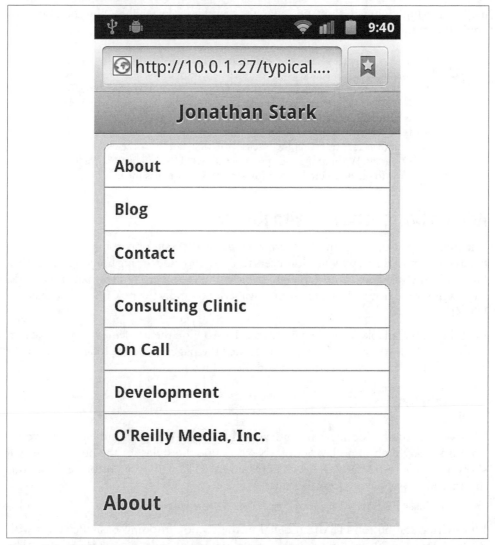

Figure 2-7. Gradients, text shadows, and rounded corners start to transform your web page into a native-looking Android app

It would be cool if you could just apply the border radius to the enclosing ul, but it doesn't work. If you try it, you'll see that the square corners of the child list items will overflow the rounded corners of the ul, thereby negating the effect.

Technically, we could achieve the rounded list effect by applying the radius corners to the ul, if we set the background color of the ul to white and set the background of its child elements to transparent. However, when users click the first or last items in the list, the tap highlight will show up squared-off and it looks terrible. Your best bet is to apply the rounding to the a tags themselves as I've demonstrated here.

 The occurrences of :first-child and :last-child above are called *pseudoclasses*. Pseudoclasses are a special type of CSS selector that allow you to target elements that meet certain implicit contextual criteria. In other words, you can style things based on characteristics—such as where they are in a list, whether they have cursor focus, or if they have been clicked—without having to manually update your markup. For example, li:first-child will select the first li that is the child of its ul parent. Without the code pseudoclass, we'd have to manually add a class to the first li to let the browser know that it was the first one.

Adding Basic Behavior with jQuery

The next step is to add some JavaScript to the page to support some basic dynamic behavior. In particular, we will allow users to show and hide the big honking navigation section in the header so that they only see it when they want to. To make this work, we'll write some new CSS and use some JavaScript to apply the new CSS to the existing HTML.

First, let's take a look at the new CSS. Step 1 is to hide the ul elements in the header so they don't show up when the user first loads the page. If you are following along at home, open your *android.css* file and add the following:

```
#header ul.hide {
    display: none;
}
```

This won't actually hide anything until you add the hide class to the ul elements (you'll do this shortly with some JavaScript). Next, define the styles for the button that will show and hide the menu. We haven't created the HTML for the button yet. For your information, it's going to look like this:

```
<div class="leftButton" onclick="toggleMenu()">Menu</div>
```

I'll describe the button HTML in detail in the section "Adding Basic Behavior with jQuery" on page 30, so don't add the preceding line of code to your HTML file. The important thing to understand is that it's a div with the class leftButton and it's going to be in the header.

Here is the CSS style for the button (you can go ahead and add this to the *android.css* file):

```
#header div.leftButton {
    position: absolute;❶
    top: 7px;
    left: 6px;
    height: 30px;❷
    font-weight: bold;❸
```

```
        text-align: center;
        color: white;
        text-shadow: rgba❹(0,0,0,0.6) 0px -1px 1px;
        line-height: 28px;❺
        border-width: 0 8px 0 8px;❻
        -webkit-border-image: url(images/button.png) 0 8 0 8;❼
}
```

 For the graphics used in this chapter, you can download the example files from the book's catalog page (see the section "How to Contact Us" on page xii) and copy them from the *images* directory. Put these copies into an *images* subdirectory beneath the directory that contains your HTML document (you'll probably need to create the *images* directory). We'll be talking about jQTouch in detail in Chapter 4.

❶ Taking it from the top, set the position to absolute to remove the `div` from the document flow. This allows you to set its top and left pixel coordinates.

❷ Set the height to 30px so it's big enough to tap easily.

❸ Style the text bold, white with a slight drop shadow, and centered in the box.

❹ In CSS, the `rgb` function is an alternative to the familiar hex notation typically used to specify colors (e.g., #FFFFFF). `rgb(255, 255, 255)` and `rgb(100%, 100%, 100%)` are both the same as #FFFFFF. More recently, the `rgba()` function has been introduced, which allows you to specify a fourth parameter that defines the *alpha value* (i.e., opacity) of the color. The range of allowable values is 0 to 1, where 0 is fully transparent and 1 is fully opaque; decimal values between 0 and 1 will be rendered translucent.

❺ The `line-height` declaration moves the text down vertically in the box so it's not flush against the top border.

❻ The `border-width` and `-webkit-border-image` lines require a bit of explanation. These two properties together allow you to assign portions of a single image to the border area of an element. If the box resizes because the text increases or decreases, the border image will stretch to accommodate it. It's really a great thing because it means fewer images, less work, less bandwidth, and shorter load times.

The `border-width` line tells the browser to apply a 0 width border to the top, an 8px border to the right, a 0 width border to the bottom, and an 8px width border to the left (i.e., the four parameters start at the top of the box and work their way around clockwise). You don't need to specify a color or style for the border.

❼ With the border widths in place, you can apply the border image. The five parameters from left to right are: the URL of the image, the top width, the right width, the bottom width, and the left width (again, clockwise from top). The URL can be absolute (*http://example.com/myBorderImage.png*) or relative. Relative paths are based on the location of the stylesheet, not the HTML page that includes the stylesheet.

When I first encountered the `border-image` property, I found it odd that I had to specify the border widths when I had already done so with the `border-width` property. After some painful trial and error, I discovered that the widths in the `border-image` property are not border widths; they are the widths *to slice* from the image. Taking the right border as an example, I'm telling the browser to take the left 8px of the image and apply them to the right border, which also happens to have an 8px width.

It is possible to do something irrational such as applying the right 4 pixels of an image to a border that is 20px wide. To make this work properly, you have to use the optional parameters of `webkit-border-image` that instruct the image what to do with the slice in the available border space (repeat, stretch, round, etc.). In three years of trying, I have failed to come up with any sane reason to do this, so I won't waste space here describing this confusing and impractical option of an otherwise killer feature.

Okay, time for some JavaScript. In preparation for the JavaScript you're about to write, you need to update your HTML document to include *jquery.js* and *android.js*. Add these lines to the `head` section of your HTML document:

```
<script type="text/javascript" src="jquery.js"></script>
<script type="text/javascript" src="android.js"></script>
```

jQuery downloads, documentation, and tutorials are available at *http://jquery.com*. To use jQuery, you will need to download it from there, rename the file you downloaded (such as *jquery-1.7.1.min.js*) to *jquery.js*, and put a copy of it in the same directory as your HTML document.

The primary duty of the JavaScript in *android.js* is to allow users to show and hide the nav menus. Copy the following JavaScript into a file called *android.js* and save it in the same folder as the HTML file:

```
if (window.innerWidth && window.innerWidth <= 600) { ❶
    $(document).ready(function(){ ❷
        $('#header ul').addClass('hide'); ❸
        $('#header').append(
            '<div class="leftButton" onclick="toggleMenu()">Menu</div>'); ❹
    });
    function toggleMenu() {
        $('#header ul').toggleClass('hide'); ❺
        $('#header .leftButton').toggleClass('pressed'); ❻
    }
}
```

❶ The entire block of code is wrapped in an `if` statement that checks to make sure the `innerWidth` property of the `window` object exists (it doesn't exist in some versions of Internet Explorer) and that the width is less than or equal to 600px (a reasonable maximum width for the most phones). By adding this line, we ensure that the code executes only when the user is browsing the page with a typical Android phone or some other similarly sized device.

 If you are testing your Android web pages using the desktop version of Chrome as described in "Don't Have a Website?" on page 13, the `if` statement here will evaluate to false if your browser's window width is too large. Manually resize your window to be as narrow as possible and refresh the page.

❷ Here we have the so-called `document ready` function. If you are new to jQuery, this can be a bit intimidating, and I admit that it took me a while to memorize the syntax. However, it's worth taking the time to commit it to memory, because you'll be using it a lot. The `document ready` function basically says, "When the document is ready, run this code." More on why this is important in a sec.

❸ This is typical jQuery code that begins by selecting the `ul`s in the header and adding the `hide` CSS class to them. Remember, `hide` is the selector we used in the CSS above. The net effect of executing this line is to, well, "hide" the header `ul` elements.

 Had we not wrapped this line in the `document ready` function, it would have most likely executed before the `ul`s were even finished loading. This means the JavaScript would load, and this line would fail because the `ul`s wouldn't exist yet. Then, the page would continue loading, the `ul`s would appear, and you'd be scratching your head (or smashing your keyboard), wondering why the JavaScript wasn't working.

❹ Here is where we append a button to the header that will allow the user to show and hide the menu (Figure 2-8). It has a class that corresponds to the CSS we wrote previously for `.leftButton`, and it has an `onclick` handler that calls the function `toggleMenu()` that comes next.

❺ The `toggleMenu()`function uses jQuery's `toggleClass()` function to add or remove the specified class to the selected object. On this line, we toggle the `hide` class on the header `ul`s.

❻ Here, we toggle the `pressed` class on the header `leftButton`.

Come to think of it, we haven't written the CSS for the `pressed` class yet, so let's do so now. Go back to *android.css* and insert the following:

```
#header div.pressed {
    -webkit-border-image: url(images/button_clicked.png) 0 8 0 8;
}
```

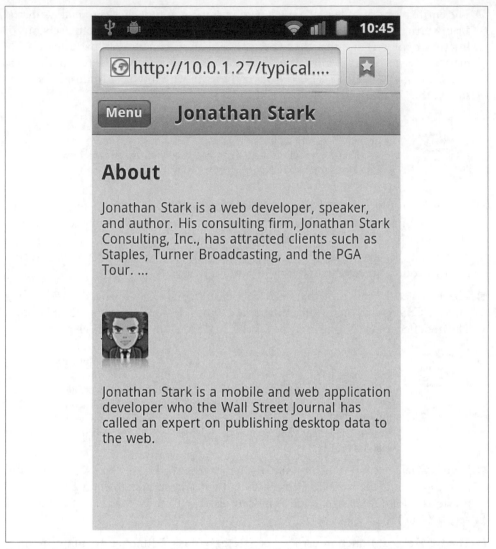

Figure 2-8. The Menu button has been added to the toolbar dynamically using jQuery

As you can see, we're simply specifying a different image for the button border (it happens to be slightly darker). This will add a two-state effect to the button that should make it evident to the user that the button can both show and hide the menu (see Figure 2-9). Figure 2-10 shows a stretched-out view of the page showing both the menu and some of the text.

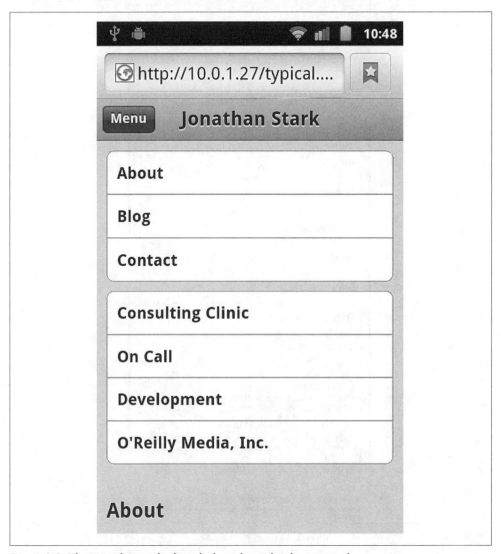

Figure 2-9. The Menu button displays darker when it has been pressed

What You've Learned

In this chapter, we covered the basics of converting an existing web page to a more Android-friendly format. We even used a bit of dynamic HTML to show and hide the navigation panels. In the next chapter, we'll build on these examples while exploring some more advanced JavaScript concepts; in particular, some yummy Ajax goodness.

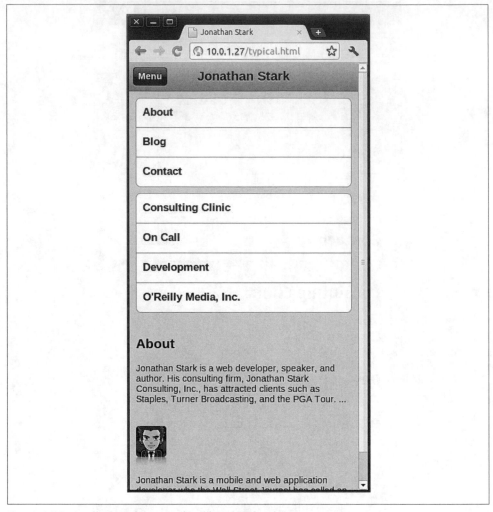

Figure 2-10. A tall view of the completed basic Android CSS

CHAPTER 3

Advanced Styling

In our quest to build an Android app without Java, we've discussed how to use CSS to style a collection of HTML pages to *look* like an Android app. In this chapter, we'll lay the groundwork to make those same pages *behave* like an Android app. Specifically, we'll discuss:

- Using Ajax to turn a full website into a single-page app.
- Creating a Back button with history using JavaScript.
- Saving the app as an icon on the home screen.

Adding a Touch of Ajax

The term Ajax (Asynchronous JavaScript and XML) has become such a buzzword that I'm not even sure I know what it means anymore. For the purposes of this book, I'm going to use the term Ajax to refer to the technique of using JavaScript to send requests to a web server without reloading the current page (e.g., to retrieve some HTML, submit a form). This approach makes for a very smooth user experience, but does require that you reinvent a lot of wheels.

For example, if you are loading external pages dynamically, the browser will not give any indication of progress or errors to the users. Furthermore, the Back button will not work as expected unless you take pains to support it. In other words, you have to do a lot of work to make a sweet Ajax app. That said, the extra effort can really pay off, because Ajax allows you to create a much richer user experience.

Traffic Cop

For the next series of examples, we'll write a single page called *android.html* that will sit in front of all the site's other pages. Here's how it works:

1. On first load, *android.html* will present the user with a nicely formatted version of the site navigation.

2. We'll then use jQuery to "hijack" the onclick actions of the nav links, so when the user clicks a link, the browser page will *not* navigate to the target link. Rather, jQuery will load a portion of the HTML from the remote page and deliver the data to the user by updating the current page.

We'll start with the most basic functional version of the code and improve it as we go along. If you've still got example files hanging around from Chapter 2, either move them out of the way or set up a new empty subdirectory on your web server to work in as you make your way through this chapter.

The HTML for the *android.html* wrapper page is extremely simple (see Example 3-1). In the head section, set the title and viewport options and include links to a stylesheet (*android.css*) and two JavaScript files: *jquery.js* and a custom JavaScript file named *android.js*.

 You must put a copy of *jquery.js* in the same directory as the HTML file. For more information on where to get *jquery.js* and what to do with it, see "Introduction to JavaScript" on page 11. You should do this now before proceeding further.

The body has just two div containers: a header with the initial title in an h1 tag and an empty div container, which will end up holding HTML snippets retrieved from other pages.

Example 3-1. This simple HTML wrapper markup will sit in front of the rest of the site's pages

```
<html>
<head>
    <title>Jonathan Stark</title>
    <meta name="viewport" content="user-scalable=no, width=device-width" />
    <link rel="stylesheet" href="android.css" type="text/css" media="screen" />
    <script type="text/javascript" src="jquery.js"></script>
    <script type="text/javascript" src="android.js"></script>
</head>
<body>
    <div id="header"><h1>Jonathan Stark</h1></div>
    <div id="container"></div>
</body>
</html>
```

Let's move on to the *android.css* file. As you can see in Example 3-2, we're going to shuffle some of the properties from previous examples in Chapter 2 (e.g., some of the `#header` `h1` properties have been moved up to `#header`), but overall everything should look familiar (if not, please review Chapter 2).

Example 3-2. The base CSS for the page is just a slightly shuffled version of previous examples

```css
body {
    background-color: #ddd;
    color: #222;
    font-family: Helvetica;
    font-size: 14px;
    margin: 0;
    padding: 0;
}
#header {
    background-color: #ccc;
    background-image: -webkit-gradient(linear, left top, left bottom,
        from(#ccc), to(#999));
    border-color: #666;
    border-style: solid;
    border-width: 0 0 1px 0;
}
#header h1 {
    color: #222;
    font-size: 20px;
    font-weight: bold;
    margin: 0 auto;
    padding: 10px 0;
    text-align: center;
    text-shadow: 0px 1px 1px #fff;
}
ul {
    list-style: none;
    margin: 10px;
    padding: 0;
}
ul li a {
    background-color: #FFF;
    border: 1px solid #999;
    color: #222;
    display: block;
    font-size: 17px;
    font-weight: bold;
    margin-bottom: -1px;
    padding: 12px 10px;
    text-decoration: none;
}
ul li:first-child a {
    -webkit-border-top-left-radius: 8px;
    -webkit-border-top-right-radius: 8px;
}
ul li:last-child a {
    -webkit-border-bottom-left-radius: 8px;
    -webkit-border-bottom-right-radius: 8px;
```

```
}
ul li a:active,ul li a:hover {
    background-color:blue;
    color:white;
}
#content {
    padding: 10px;
    text-shadow: 0px 1px 1px #fff;
}
#content a {
    color: blue;
}
```

Setting Up Some Content to Work With

This JavaScript loads a document called *index.html*, and will not work without it. Before you proceed, copy the HTML file from Example 2-1 into the same directory as *android.html*, and rename it *index.html*. However, none of the links in it will work unless the targets of the links actually exist. You can create these files yourself or download the example code from this book's website (see "How to Contact Us" on page xii).

 If you want a few functioning links to play with, you can create *about.html*, *blog.html*, and *consulting-clinic.html*. To do so, just duplicate *index.html* a few times and change the filename of each copy to match the related link. For added effect, you can change the content of the h2 tag in each file to match the filename. For example, the h2 in *blog.html* would be <h2>Blog</h2>.

At this point, you should have the following files in your working directory:

android.html
    You created this in Example 3-1.

android.css
    You created this in Example 3-2.

index.html
    A copy of the HTML file from Example 2-1.

about.html
    A copy of *index.html*, with the h2 set to "About".

blog.html
    A copy of *index.html*, with the h2 set to "Blog".

consulting-clinic.html
    A copy of *index.html*, with the h2 set to "Consulting Clinic".

Routing Requests with JavaScript

The JavaScript in *android.js* is where all the magic happens in this example. Create this file in the same directory as your *android.html* file. Please refer to Example 3-3 as we go through it line by line.

Example 3-3. This bit of JavaScript in android.js converts the links on the page to Ajax requests

```javascript
$(document).ready(function(){ ❶
    loadPage();
});
function loadPage(url) {❷
    if (url == undefined) {
        $('#container').load('index.html #header ul', hijackLinks);❸
    } else {
        $('#container').load(url + ' #content', hijackLinks);❹
    }
}
function hijackLinks() {❺
    $('#container a').click(function(e){❻
        e.preventDefault();❼
        loadPage(e.target.href);❽
    });
}
```

❶ Here we're using jQuery's `document ready` function to have the browser run the `loadPage()` function when the browser has finished constructing the page.

❷ The `loadPage()` function accepts a single parameter called `url` and then checks (on the next line) whether a value has been sent.

❸ If a value is not sent into the function (as will be the case when it is called for the first time from the `document ready` function), `url` will be undefined and this line will execute. This line and the following are examples of jQuery's `load()` function. The `load()` function is excellent for adding quick and dirty Ajax functionality to a page. If this line were translated into English, it would read, "Get all of the `ul` elements from the `#header` element of `index.html` and insert them into the `#container` element of the current page. When you're done, run the `hijackLinks()` function."

 index.html refers to the home page of the site. If your home page is named differently, you'd use that filename here instead. If you've been following the instructions in this chapter exactly, you used *index.html*.

❹ This line is executed if the `url` parameter has a value. It says, in effect, "Get the `#content` element from the `url` that was passed into the `loadPage()` function and insert it into the `#container` element of the current page. When you're done, run the `hijackLinks()` function."

❺ Once the `load()` function has completed, the `#container` element of the current page will contain the HTML snippet that was retrieved. Then, `load()` will run the `hijackLinks()` function.

❻ On this line, `hijackLinks()` finds all of the links in that new snippet of HTML and binds a click handler to them using the lines of code that follow. Click handlers are automatically passed an event object, which we're capturing as the function parameter `e`. The event object of a clicked link contains the URL of the remote page in `e.target.href`.

❼ Normally, a web browser will navigate to a new page when the user clicks a link. This navigation response is called the *default behavior* of the link. Since we are handling clicks and loading pages through JavaScript, we need to prevent this default behavior. On this line, which (along with the next line) is triggered when a user clicks one of the links, call the built-in `preventDefault()` method of the event object. If we leave that line out, the browser will dutifully leave the current page and navigate to the URL of clicked link.

❽ When the user clicks, pass the URL of the remote page to the `loadPage()` function, and the cycle starts all over again.

One of my favorite things about JavaScript is that you can pass a function as a parameter to another function. Although this looks weird at first, it's extremely powerful and allows you to make your code modular and reusable. If you'd like to learn more, you should check out *JavaScript: The Good Parts* by Douglas Crockford (O'Reilly). In fact, if you are working with JavaScript, you should check out everything by Douglas Crockford; you'll be glad you did.

Click handlers do not run when the page first loads; they run when the user actually clicks a link. Assigning click handlers is like setting booby traps; you do some initial setup work for something that may or may not be triggered later.

It's worth taking a few minutes to read up on the properties of the event object that JavaScript creates in response to user actions in the browser. A good reference is located at *http://www.w3schools.com/htmldom/dom_obj_event.asp*.

When testing the code in this chapter, be sure you point your browser at the *android.html* page. Web servers will typically default to displaying *index.html* if you just navigate to the directory that the files are in. Normally this is helpful, but in this case it will cause a problem.

Simple Bells and Whistles

With this tiny bit of HTML, CSS, and JavaScript, we have essentially turned an entire website into a single-page application. However, it still leaves quite a bit to be desired. Let's slick things up a bit.

Progress Indicator

Since we are not allowing the browser to navigate from page to page, the user will not see any indication of progress while data is loading. We need to provide some feedback to users to let them know that something is, in fact, happening (Figure 3-1). Without this feedback, users may wonder if they actually clicked the link or missed it, and will often start clicking all over the place in frustration. This can lead to increased server load and application instability (i.e., crashing).

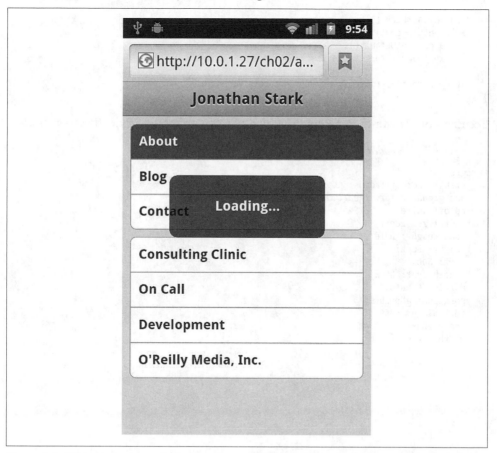

Figure 3-1. Without a progress indicator of some kind, your app will seem unresponsive and your users will get frustrated

Thanks to jQuery, providing a progress indicator only takes two lines of code. We'll just append a loading `div` to the body when `loadPage()` starts and remove the loading `div` when `hijackLinks()` is done. Example 3-4 shows a modified version of Example 3-3. The lines you need to add to *android.js* are shown in bold.

Example 3-4. Adding a simple progress indicator to the page

```
$(document).ready(function(){
    loadPage();
});
function loadPage(url) {
    $('body').append('<div id="progress">Loading...</div>');
    if (url == undefined) {
        $('#container').load('index.html #header ul', hijackLinks);
    } else {
        $('#container').load(url + ' #content', hijackLinks);
    }
}
function hijackLinks() {
    $('#container a').click(function(e){
        e.preventDefault();
        loadPage(e.target.href);
    });
    $('#progress').remove();
}
```

See Example 3-5 for the CSS you need to add to *android.css* to style the progress `div`.

Example 3-5. CSS added to android.css used to style the progress indicator

```
#progress {
    -webkit-border-radius: 10px;
    background-color: rgba(0,0,0,.7);
    color: white;
    font-size: 18px;
    font-weight: bold;
    height: 80px;
    left: 60px;
    line-height: 80px;
    margin: 0 auto;
    position: absolute;
    text-align: center;
    top: 120px;
    width: 200px;
}
```

Simulating Real-World Network Performance

If you are testing this web application on a local network, the network speeds will be so fast you won't ever see the progress indicator. If you are running your server on Mac OS X, you can slow all incoming web traffic by typing a couple of `ipfw` commands at the terminal. For example, these commands will slow all web traffic to 1 kilobyte per second:

```
sudo ipfw pipe 1 config bw 1KByte/s
sudo ipfw add 100 pipe 1 tcp from any to me 80
```

You should use your computer's hostname or external IP address in the URL (for example, `mycomputer.local` rather than `localhost`). When you're done testing, delete the rule with `sudo ipfw delete 100` (you can delete all custom rules with `ipfw flush`).

If you are using IIS on Windows, you can install the Bit Rate Throttling Media Services extension from *http://www.iis.net/download/BitRateThrottling*. Open the IIS Manager, select your web site, and double-click Bit Rate Throttling under the Media Services group. Using the list of actions on the right, add a throttle setting for the HTML MIME type (`text/html`) and set it to something slow (1 kbps is good). Enable Bit Rate Throttling, and your pages should be loading very slowly now. Don't forget to disable Bit Rate Throttling when you're done testing!

You can do similar things on Linux as well. For more information, check out the following links:

- *http://linux-ip.net/articles/Traffic-Control-HOWTO/classless-qdiscs.html*
- *http://lartc.org/howto/lartc.ratelimit.single.html*

But if all you want to do is to delay the JavaScript execution so the "Loading" message appears onscreen as long as possible, you can add the following lines of code to the top of the `hijackLinks()` function:

```
var stopTime = new Date().getTime() + 5000;
while (new Date().getTime() < stopTime);
```

This is not the right way to delay the execution of something in JavaScript—you should use JavaScript's `setTimeout` function for that—but this sure is a good way to make sure your JavaScript freezes and does nothing (except eat up your device's CPU) during this time. So be sure to take those lines of code out as soon as you can, or you'll be cursing the day you ever typed them in.

Setting the Page Title

Our site happens to have a single h2 at the beginning of each page that would make a nice page title (see Figure 3-2). You can see this in the HTML source shown in Chapter 2. To be more mobile-friendly, we'll pull that title out of the content and put it in the header (see Figure 3-3). Again, jQuery to the rescue: you can just add three lines to the hijackLinks() function to make it happen. Example 3-6 shows the hijackLinks function with these changes.

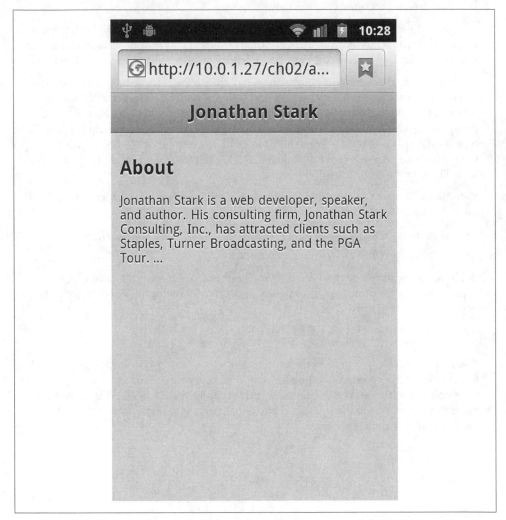

Figure 3-2. Before moving the page heading to the toolbar...

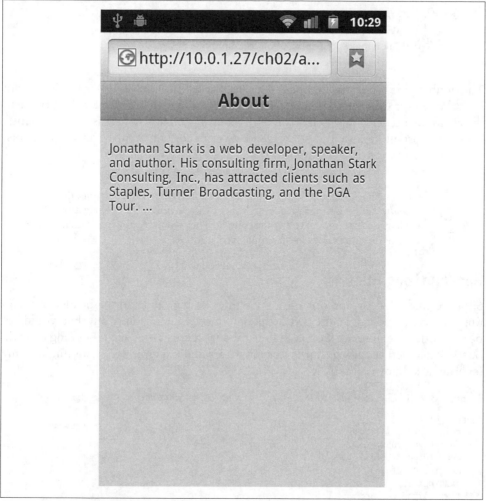

Figure 3-3. ...and after moving the page heading to the toolbar

Example 3-6. Using the h2 from the target page as the toolbar title

```
function hijackLinks() {
    $('#container a').click(function(e){
        e.preventDefault();
        loadPage(e.target.href);
    });
    var title = $('h2').html() || 'Hello!';
    $('h1').html(title);
    $('h2').remove();
    $('#progress').remove();
}
```

I added the title lines before the line that removes the progress indicator. I like to remove the progress indicator as the very last action because I think it makes the application feel more responsive.

The double pipe (||) in the first line of inserted code (shown in bold) is the JavaScript logical operator OR. Translated into English, that line reads, "Set the title variable to the HTML contents of the h2 element, or to the string 'Hello!' if there is no h2 element." This is important because the first page load won't contain an h2 because we are just grabbing the nav uls.

This point probably needs some clarification. When users first load the *android.html* URL, they are only going to see the overall site navigation elements, as opposed to any site content. They won't see any site content until they tap a link on this initial navigation page.

Handling Long Titles

Suppose we had a page on our site with a title too long to fit in the header bar (Figure 3-4). We could just let the text break onto more than one line, but that would not be very attractive. Instead, we can update the #header h1 styles such that long text will be truncated with a trailing ellipsis (see Figure 3-5 and Example 3-7). This might be my favorite little-known CSS trick.

Example 3-7. Adding an ellipsis to text that is too long for its container

```
#header h1 {
    color: #222;
    font-size: 20px;
    font-weight: bold;
    margin: 0 auto;
    padding: 10px 0;
    text-align: center;
    text-shadow: 0px 1px 1px #fff;
    max-width: 160px;
    overflow: hidden;
    white-space: nowrap;
    text-overflow: ellipsis;
}
```

Here's the rundown: max-width: 160px instructs the browser not to allow the h1 element to grow wider than 160px. Then, overflow: hidden instructs the browser to chop off any content that extends outside the element borders. Next, white-space: nowrap prevents the browser from breaking the line into two. Without this line, the h1 would just get taller to accommodate the text at the defined width. Finally, text-overflow: ellipsis appends three dots to the end of any chopped-off text to indicate to the user that she is not seeing the entire string.

Figure 3-4. Text wrapping in the toolbar is not very attractive...

Automatic Scroll-to-Top

Let's say you have a page that is longer than the viewable area on the phone. The user visits the page, scrolls down to the bottom, and clicks on a link to an even longer page. In this case, the new page will show up "prescrolled" instead of at the top as you'd expect.

Technically, this makes sense because we are not actually leaving the current (scrolled) page, but it's certainly a confusing situation for the user. To rectify the situation, we can add a `scrollTo()` command to the `loadPage()` function (Example 3-8).

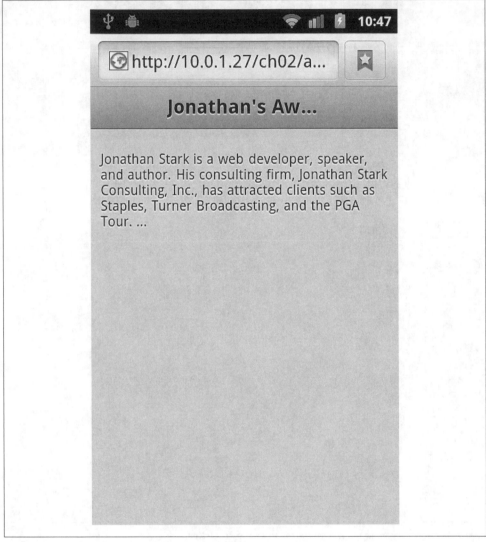

Figure 3-5. …but we can beautify it with a CSS ellipsis

Whenever a user clicks a link, the page will first jump to the top. This has the added benefit of ensuring the loading graphic is visible if the user clicks a link at the bottom of a long page.

Example 3-8. It's a good idea to scroll back to the top when a user navigates to a new page

```
function loadPage(url) {
    $('body').append('<div id="progress">Loading...</div>');
    scrollTo(0,0);
```

```
        if (url == undefined) {
            $('#container').load('index.html #header ul', hijackLinks);
        } else {
            $('#container').load(url + ' #content', hijackLinks);
        }
}
```

Hijacking Local Links Only

Like most sites, ours has links to external pages (i.e., pages hosted on other domains). We shouldn't hijack these external links, because it wouldn't make sense to inject their HTML into our Android-specific layout. As shown in Example 3-9, we can add a conditional that checks the destination URL to see if it matches the domain name that the page was loaded from. If it matches, the link is hijacked and the content is loaded into the current page (i.e., Ajax is in effect). If not, the browser will navigate to the URL normally.

Example 3-9. You can allow external pages to load normally by checking the domain name of the URL

```
function hijackLinks() {
    $('#container a').click(function(e){
        var url = e.target.href;
        if (url.match(window.location.hostname)) {
            e.preventDefault();
            loadPage(url);
        }
    });
    var title = $('h2').html() || 'Hello!';
    $('h1').html(title);
    $('h2').remove();
    $('#progress').remove();
}
```

 The `url.match` function uses a language, regular expressions, that is often embedded within other programming languages such as JavaScript, PHP, and Perl. Although this regular expression is simple, more complex expressions can be a bit intimidating, but are well worth becoming familiar with. My favorite regex page is located at *http://www .regular-expressions.info/javascriptexample.html*.

Roll Your Own Back Button

The elephant in the room at this point is that the user has no way to navigate back to previous pages (remember that we've hijacked all the links, so the browser page history won't work). Let's address that by adding a Back button to the top left corner of the screen. First, we'll update the JavaScript, and then we'll do the CSS.

Adding a standard toolbar Back button to the app means keeping track of the user's click history. To do this, we'll have to:

- Store the URL of the previous page so we know where to go back to
- Store the title of the previous page so we know what label to put on the Back button

Adding this feature touches on most of the JavaScript we've written so far in this chapter, so I'll go over the entire new version of *android.js* line by line (see Example 3-10), and then show you the CSS you need to support it. The result will look like Figure 3-6.

Example 3-10. Expanding the existing JavaScript example to include support for a Back button

```
var hist = [];❶
var startUrl = 'index.html';❷
$(document).ready(function(){❸
    loadPage(startUrl);
});
function loadPage(url) {
    $('body').append('<div id="progress">Loading...</div>');❹
    scrollTo(0,0);
    if (url == startUrl) {❺
        var element = ' #header ul';
    } else {
        var element = ' #content';
    }
    $('#container').load(url + element, function(){❻
        var title = $('h2').html() || 'Hello!';
        $('h1').html(title);
        $('h2').remove();
        $('.leftButton').remove();❼
        hist.unshift({'url':url, 'title':title});❽
        if (hist.length > 1) {❾
            $('#header').append('<div class="leftButton">'+hist[1].title+'</div>');❿
            $('#header .leftButton').click(function(){⓫
                var thisPage = hist.shift();⓬
                var previousPage = hist.shift();
                loadPage(previousPage.url);
            });
        }
        $('#container a').click(function(e){⓭
            var url = e.target.href;
            if (url.match(window.location.hostname)) {⓮
                e.preventDefault();
                loadPage(url);
            }
        });
        $('#progress').remove();
    });
}
```

❶ This line initializes a variable named hist as an empty array. Since it is defined outside of any functions, it exists in the global scope and will be available everywhere in the page. Notice that it doesn't use the full word history as the variable name, because that is a predefined object property in JavaScript and you should avoid it in your own code.

❷ This line defines the relative URL of the remote page to load when the user first visits *android.html*. You might recall that earlier examples checked for `url == undefined` to handle the first page load, but in this example we are using the start page in a few places. Therefore, it makes sense to define it globally.

❸ This line and the next make up the `document ready` function definition. Unlike previous examples, we're passing the start page to the `loadPage()` function.

❹ On to the `loadPage()` function. This line and the next are verbatim from previous examples.

❺ This `if...else` statement determines which elements to load from the remote page. For example, if we want the start page, we grab the `ul`s from the header; otherwise, we grab the content `div`.

❻ On this line, the `url` parameter and the appropriate source element are concatenated as the first parameter passed to the load function. As for the second parameter, we're passing an *anonymous function* (an unnamed function that is defined inline) directly. As we go through the anonymous function, you'll notice a strong resemblance to the `hijackLinks()` function, which has been replaced by this anonymous function. For example, the following three lines are identical to previous examples.

❼ On this line, we remove the `.leftButton` object from the page. This might seem weird because we haven't yet added it to the page; we'll be adding it a couple steps down.

❽ Here we use the built-in `unshift` method of the JavaScript array to add an object to the beginning of the `hist` array. The object has two properties: `url` and `title`—the two pieces of information we need to support the Back button display and behavior.

❾ This line includes the built-in `length` method of the JavaScript array to find out how many objects are in the history array. If there is only one object in the history array, it means the user is on the first page. Therefore, we don't need to display a Back button. However, if there is more than one object in the hist array, we need to add a button to the header.

❿ This line adds the `.leftButton` I mentioned above. The text of the button will be the same as the title of the page before the current page, which is what we're accessing with the `hist[1].title` code. JavaScript arrays are zero-based, so the first item in the array (the current page) has an index of 0. In other words, index 0 is the current page, index 1 is the previous page, index 2 is the page before that, and so on.

⓫ This block of code binds an anonymous function to the click handler of the Back button. Remember, click handler code executes when the user clicks, not when the page loads. So, after the page loads and the user clicks to go back, the code inside this function will run.

⓬ This line and the next use the built-in `shift` method of the array to remove the first two items from the `hist` array, then the last line in the function sends the URL of the previous page to the `loadPage()` function.

⓭ The remaining lines were copied exactly from previous examples, so I won't rehash them here.

⓮ This is the URL-matching code introduced earlier in this chapter.

 Please go visit *http://www.hunlock.com/blogs/Mastering_Javascript_Ar rays* for a full listing of JavaScript array functions with descriptions and examples.

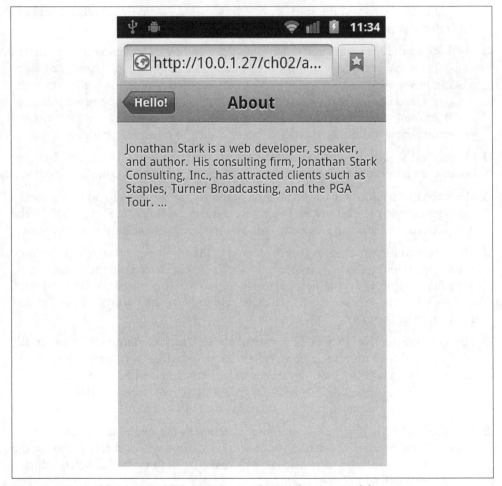

Figure 3-6. It wouldn't be a mobile app without a glossy, left-arrow Back button

Now that we have our Back button, all that remains is to purty it up with some CSS (see Example 3-11). We'll start off by styling the text with `font-weight`, `text-align`, `line-height`, `color`, and `text-shadow`. We'll continue by placing the `div` precisely where we want it on the page with `position`, `top`, and `left`. Then, we'll make sure that long text on the button label will truncate with an ellipsis using `max-width`, `white-space`, `overflow`, and `text-overflow`. Finally, we'll apply a graphic with `border-width` and `-webkit-border-image`. Unlike the earlier border image example, this image has a different width for the left and right borders because the image is made asymmetrical by the arrowhead on the left side.

 Don't forget that you'll need an image for this button. You'll need to save it as *back_button.png* in the *images* folder underneath the folder that holds your HTML file. See "Adding Basic Behavior with jQuery" on page 29 for tips on finding or creating your own button images.

Example 3-11. Add the following to android.css to beautify the Back button with a border image

```
#header div.leftButton {
    font-weight: bold;
    text-align: center;
    line-height: 28px;
    color: white;
    text-shadow: 0px -1px 1px rgba(0,0,0,0.6);
    position: absolute;
    top: 7px;
    left: 6px;
    max-width: 50px;
    white-space: nowrap;
    overflow: hidden;
    text-overflow: ellipsis;
    border-width: 0 8px 0 14px;
    -webkit-border-image: url(images/back_button.png) 0 8 0 14;
}
```

By default, Android displays an orange highlight on clickable objects that have been tapped (Figure 3-7). This may appear only briefly, but removing it is easy and makes the app look much better. Fortunately, Android supports a CSS property called `-webkit-tap-highlight-color`, which allows you to suppress this behavior. We can do this here by setting the tap highlight to a fully transparent color (see Example 3-12).

Example 3-12. Add the following to android.css to remove the default tap highlight effect

```
#header div.leftButton {
    font-weight: bold;
    text-align: center;
    line-height: 28px;
    color: white;
    text-shadow: 0px -1px 1px rgba(0,0,0,0.6);
```

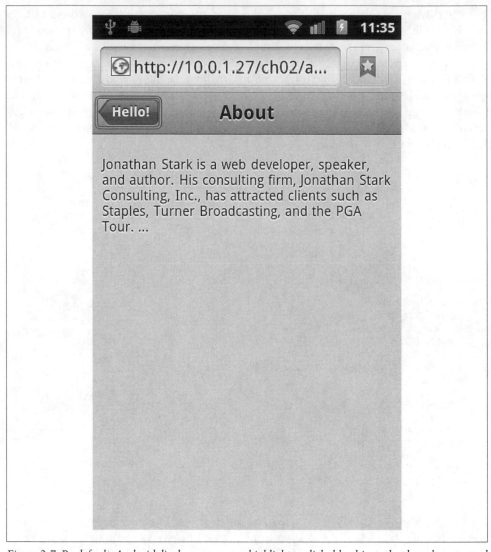

Figure 3-7. By default, Android displays an orange highlight to clickable objects that have been tapped

```
    position: absolute;
    top: 7px;
    left: 6px;
    max-width: 50px;
    white-space: nowrap;
    overflow: hidden;
    text-overflow: ellipsis;
    border-width: 0 8px 0 14px;
    -webkit-border-image: url(images/back_button.png) 0 8 0 14;
    -webkit-tap-highlight-color: rgba(0,0,0,0);
}
```

In the case of the Back button, there could be at least a second or two of delay before the content from the previous page appears. To avoid frustration, we can configure the button to look clicked the instant it's tapped. In a desktop browser, this is a simple process: you just add a declaration to your CSS using the `:active` pseudoclass to specify an alternate style for the object that the user clicked. I don't know if it's a bug or a feature, but this approach does not work on Android; the `:active` style is ignored.

I toyed around with combinations of `:active` and `:hover`, which brought me some success with non-Ajax apps. However, with an Ajax app like the one we are using here, the `:hover` style is sticky (i.e., the button appears to remain "clicked" even after the finger is removed).

Fortunately, the fix is pretty simple—use jQuery to add the class `clicked` to the button when the user taps it. I've opted to apply a darker version of the button image to the button in the example (see Figure 3-8 and Example 3-13). You'll need to make sure you have a button image called *back_button_clicked.png* in the *images* subfolder. See "Adding Basic Behavior with jQuery" on page 29 for tips on finding or creating your own button images.

Example 3-13. Add the following to android.css to make the Back button looked clicked when the user taps it

```
#header div.leftButton.clicked {
    -webkit-border-image: url(images/back_button_clicked.png) 0 8 0 14;
}
```

 Since we're using an image for the clicked style, it would be smart to preload the image. Otherwise, the unclicked button graphic will disappear the first time it's tapped while the clicked graphic downloads. I'll cover image preloading in the next chapter.

With the CSS in place, we can now update the portion of the *android.js* that assigns the click handler to the Back button. First, we add a variable, e, to the anonymous function to capture the incoming click event. Then, we wrap the event target in a jQuery selector and call jQuery's `addClass()` function to assign the clicked CSS class to the button:

```
$('#header .leftButton').click(function(e){
    $(e.target).addClass('clicked');
    var thisPage = hist.shift();
    var previousPage = hist.shift();
    loadPage(lastUrl.url);
});
```

 A special note to any CSS gurus in the crowd: the CSS Sprite technique—popularized by A List Apart—is not an option in this case because it requires setting offsets for the image. The `-webkit-border-image` property does not support image offsets.

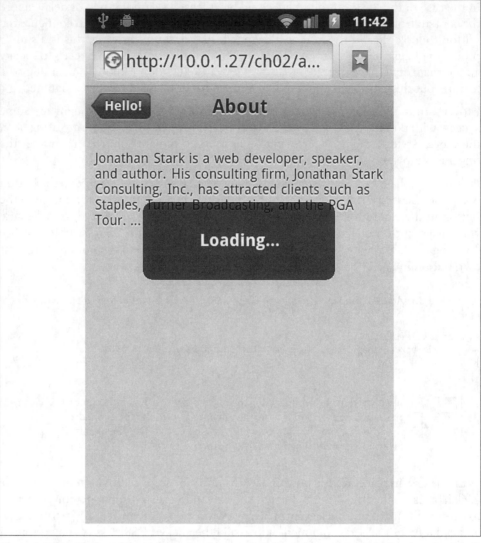

Figure 3-8. It might be tough to tell in print, but the clicked Back button is a bit darker than the default state

Adding an Icon to the Home Screen

Hopefully, users will want to add an icon for your web app to their home screens (this is called a "launcher icon"). They do this by bookmarking your app and adding a bookmark shortcut to their home screens. This is the same process they use to add any bookmark to their home screens. The difference is that we're going to specify a custom image to display in place of the default bookmark icon.

First, upload a *.png* image file to your website. To maintain a consistent visual weight with other launcher icons, it's recommended that the file be 56px × 56px if its visible area is basically square, and 60px × 60px otherwise. You'll have to experiment with your specific graphic to settle on the perfect dimensions.

Because Android is built to run on many different devices with a variety of screen sizes and pixel densities, creating icons that look good everywhere is fairly involved. For detailed instructions and free downloadable templates, please visit the Icon Design page on the Android developer site (*http://developer.android.com/guide/practices/ui_guidelines/icon_de sign.html#launcherstructure*).

Next, add the following line to the head section of the "traffic cop" HTML document (*android.html*), *android.html* (replace myCustomIcon.png with the absolute or relative path to the image):

```
<link rel="apple-touch-icon-precomposed" href="myCustomIcon.png" />
```

As you might have noticed, this is an Apple-specific directive that has been adopted by Android.

What You've Learned

In this chapter, you've learned how to convert a normal website into an Ajax application, complete with progress indicators and a native-looking Back button. In the next chapter, you'll learn how to make your app come alive by adding native UI animations. That's right; here comes the fun stuff!

CHAPTER 4

Animation

Android apps have a number of distinctive animation characteristics that add context and meaning for the user. For example, pages slide left as users drill down through links, and slide right as they navigate back. In this chapter, you'll learn how to add characteristic behaviors like sliding, page flip, and more to your web app. These changes will make your web app almost indistinguishable from a native application.

With a Little Help from Our Friend

I'll be honest: making a web page animate like a typical native app is hard. Fortunately, an enterprising young lad named David Kaneda has created a JavaScript library called jQTouch that makes mobile web development a whole heckuva lot easier. jQTouch is an open source jQuery plug-in that handles virtually everything we learned in the previous chapter, as well as a boatload of much more complex stuff that would be truly painful to write from scratch.

 At the time of this writing, the stable release of jQTouch is v1.0b3.1, which you can download at *https://github.com/senchalabs/jQTouch/zip ball/b3.1*. Some fairly significant changes are planned for the next release of jQTouch. If a newer version is available by the time you read this, you might want to stick with v1.0b3.1 while you go through the rest of the book, and upgrade to the latest version only after you are comfortable with the underlying concepts.

Sliding Home

We are going to build a simple calorie-tracking application called Kilo that allows the user to add and delete food entries for a given date. All told, there will be five panels: Home, Settings, Dates, Date, and New Entry. We'll start off with two panels and work our way up as we go.

We will be assigning CSS classes to some of the HTML elements (e.g., toolbar, edgetoedge, arrow, button, back). In every case, these classes correspond to predefined CSS class selectors that exist in the default jQTouch theme. Bear in mind that you can create and use your own classes by modifying existing jQTouch themes or creating your own from scratch; we're just using the defaults in the examples here.

We're going to start from scratch here, so you can put aside the files you created in the preceding chapters. To begin, let's create a file named *index.html* and add the HTML given in Example 4-1 for the Home and About panels.

Example 4-1. HTML for the Home and About panels in index.html

```
<html>
    <head>
        <title>Kilo</title>
    </head>
    <body>
        <div id="home">❶
            <div class="toolbar">❷
                <h1>Kilo</h1>
            </div>
            <ul class="edgetoedge">❸
                <li class="arrow"><a href="#about">About</a></li>❹
            </ul>
        </div>
        <div id="about">
            <div class="toolbar">
                <h1>About</h1>
                <a class="button back" href="#">Back</a>❺
            </div>
            <div>
                <p>Kilo gives you easy access to your food diary.</p>
            </div>
        </div>
    </body>
</html>
```

The HTML here basically amounts to a head with a title and a body with two children, both divs:

❶ This div (as well as the about div that appears a few lines down) will become a panel in the application by virtue of the fact that they are direct descendants of the body.

❷ Inside each panel div, there is a div with a class of toolbar. This toolbar class is specifically predefined in the jQTouch themes to style an element like a traditional mobile phone toolbar.

❸ This unordered list tag has the class edgetoedge. The edgetoedge class tells jQTouch to stretch the list all the way from left to right in the viewable area.

❹ On this line there is an `li` that contains a link with its `href` pointing at the About panel. Including the `arrow` class on the `li` is optional; doing so will add a chevron to the right side of the item in the list.

❺ The toolbar elements each contain a single `h1` element that will become the panel title. On this line, there are links with the classes `button` and `back`, which tell jQTouch to make the button look and act like a Back button.

 The `href` on the Back button is set to `#`. Normally, this would tell the browser to return to the top of the current document. But when using jQTouch, it navigates back to the previous panel instead. In more advanced scenarios, you might want to use a specific anchor, such as `#home`, which instructs the Back button to navigate to a particular panel regardless of what the previous panel was.

With the basic HTML in place, it's time to add jQTouch to the party. Once you've installed jQTouch into the same directory as the HTML document (see "Installing jQTouch" below), just add a few lines of code to the head of your page (Example 4-2).

Installing jQTouch

For this and other examples in this book, you will need to download jQTouch from *http://www.jqtouch.com*, unzip it, and move the *jqtouch* and *themes* directories into the same directory as your HTML document. You will also need to go into the *jqtouch* directory and rename the jQuery JavaScript file (such as *jquery.1.4.2.min.js*) to *jquery.js*.

Example 4-2. Adding these lines to the head of your document will activate jQTouch

```
<link type="text/css" rel="stylesheet" media="screen"
      href="jqtouch/jqtouch.css">❶
<link type="text/css" rel="stylesheet" media="screen"
      href="themes/jqt/theme.css">❷
<script type="text/javascript" src="jqtouch/jquery.js"></script>❸
<script type="text/javascript" src="jqtouch/jqtouch.js"></script>❹
<script type="text/javascript">❺
    var jQT = $.jQTouch({
        icon: 'kilo.png'
    });
</script>
```

❶ This line includes the *jqtouch.css* file. This file defines some hardcore structural design rules that are very specific to handling animations, orientation, and other Android-specific minutiae. This file is required and there should be no reason for you to edit it.

❷ This line specifies the CSS for the selected theme, in this case, the `jqt` theme, which comes with jQTouch. The classes that we've been using in the HTML correspond to CSS selectors in this document. jQTouch comes with two themes available by default. You can also make your own by duplicating a default theme and making changes to it or writing a new one from scratch.

❸ jQTouch requires jQuery, so it is included here. jQTouch comes with its own copy of jQuery (which you need to rename to *jquery.js*, as described earlier), but you can link to another copy if you prefer.

❹ This is where we include jQTouch itself. Notice that you have to include jQTouch after jQuery or ain't nothin' gonna work.

❺ This brings us to the script block where we initialize the jQTouch object and send in a property value: `icon`.

jQTouch exposes several properties that allow you to customize the behavior and appearance of your app. You'll see several throughout the course of this book, and they are all optional. However, you'll pretty much always be using at least a few of them.

In this case, `icon` tells jQTouch where to look for the custom home screen icon.

The difference between the application before jQTouch (Figure 4-1) and after (Figure 4-2) is dramatic, but the truly astonishing change is that you've just added gorgeous left/right sliding to your app with 10 lines of code. jQTouch is awesome, and we're just getting started.

Adding the Dates Panel

Let's add the Dates panel. The Dates panel will have a list of relative dates beginning with today and going back to five days ago. Add the HTML for the Dates panel (shown in Example 4-3) right after the About panel, just before the closing **</body>** (in a moment, I'll show you how to add a link to this from the Home panel).

Example 4-3. The HTML for the Dates panel

```
<div id="dates">
    <div class="toolbar">
        <h1>Dates</h1>
        <a class="button back" href="#">Back</a>
    </div>
    <ul class="edgetoedge">
        <li class="arrow"><a id="0" href="#date">Today</a></li>
        <li class="arrow"><a id="1" href="#date">Yesterday</a></li>
        <li class="arrow"><a id="2" href="#date">2 Days Ago</a></li>
        <li class="arrow"><a id="3" href="#date">3 Days Ago</a></li>
        <li class="arrow"><a id="4" href="#date">4 Days Ago</a></li>
        <li class="arrow"><a id="5" href="#date">5 Days Ago</a></li>
    </ul>
</div>
```

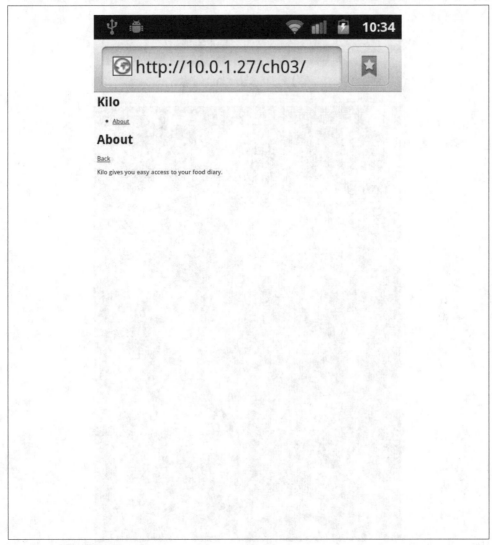

Figure 4-1. Kilo before jQTouch...

Like the About panel, the Dates panel has a toolbar with a title and Back button. After the toolbar, there is an unordered `edgetoedge` list of links. Notice that all of the links have unique IDs (i.e., 0 through 5) but the same `href` (i.e., `#date`)—more on that in a bit.

Next, you have to update the Home panel with a link to the Dates panel. Add the line shown in bold to the Home panel in *index.html*:

```
<div id="home">
    <div class="toolbar">
        <h1>Kilo</h1>
    </div>
</div>
```

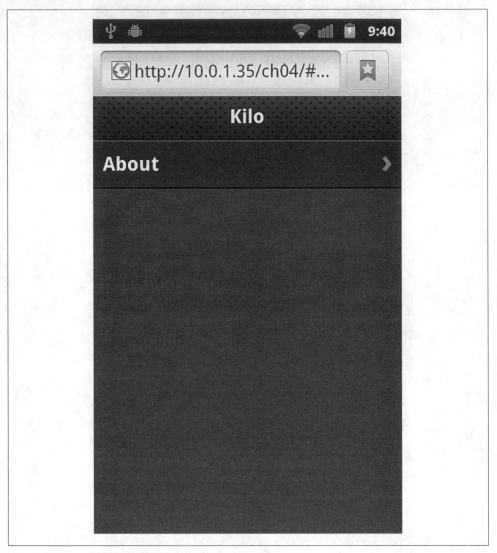

Figure 4-2. ...and Kilo after jQTouch

```
    <ul class="edgetoedge">
        <li class="arrow"><a href="#dates">Dates</a></li>
        <li class="arrow"><a href="#about">About</a></li>
    </ul>
</div>
```

And just like that, we've added a new panel to the app (Figure 4-3). If you click Dates, the Dates panel will appear, as shown in Figure 4-4. Clicking on an item on the Dates panel doesn't do anything yet. Let's rectify that situation by adding a panel to display a date item (the Date panel).

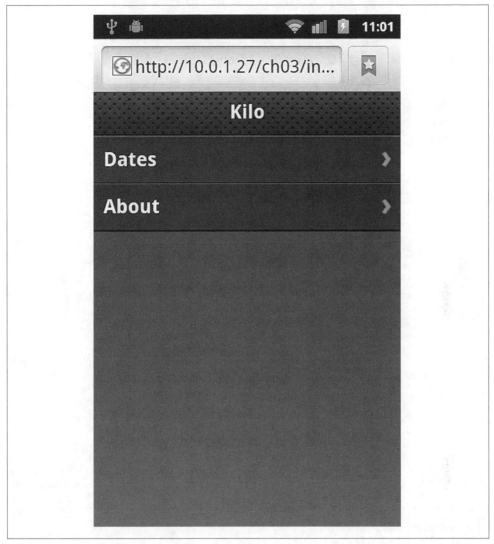

Figure 4-3. The Home panel now has a link to the Dates panel

Adding the Date Panel

The Date panel looks a lot like the previous panels, with a couple of exceptions (refer to Example 4-4). Add the HTML for the Date panel right after the Dates panel, just before the closing </body>.

Figure 4-4. The Dates panel consists of a toolbar with a Back button and a clickable list of relative dates

Example 4-4. The HTML for the Date panel

```
<div id="date">
    <div class="toolbar">
        <h1>Date</h1>
        <a class="button back" href="#">Back</a>
        <a class="button slideup" href="#createEntry">+</a>❶
    </div>
    <ul class="edgetoedge">
        <li id="entryTemplate" class="entry" style="display:none">❷
            <span class="label">Label</span>
            <span class="calories">000</span>
            <span class="delete">Delete</span>
        </li>
    </ul>
</div>
```

❶ The Date panel toolbar has an additional button. When clicked, this button will display the New Entry panel (which we have not yet built). The link has a class of `slideup`, which tells jQTouch that we want the target panel to slide up from the bottom of the screen, rather than in from the left or right like normal navigation.

❷ The other unusual aspect of this panel is that we define a list item with the style set to `display:none`, effectively making it invisible.

As you'll see in a bit, we'll use this invisible list item as a template to display entries once they are created. At this point, there are no entries, so the panel will be empty aside from the toolbar.

Now that you've added the Date panel, clicking any item on the Dates panel will slide the empty Date panel (Figure 4-5) into view.

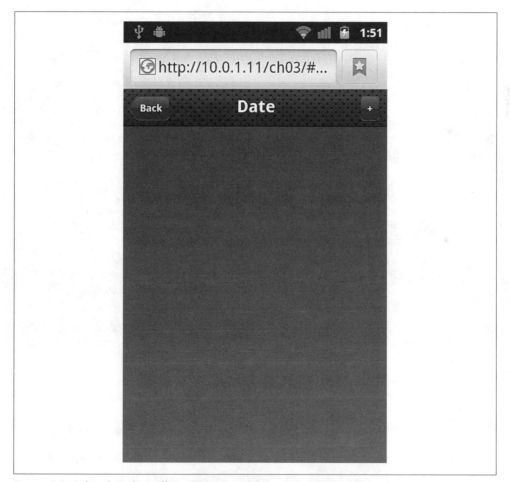

Figure 4-5. Other than the toolbar, the Date panel is empty to begin with

Adding the New Entry Panel

Example 4-5 shows the source code for the New Entry panel. Add this code to the end of *index.html*, before the closing `</body>`.

Example 4-5. The HTML for the New Entry panel

```
<div id="createEntry">
    <div class="toolbar">
        <h1>New Entry</h1>
        <a class="button cancel" href="#">Cancel</a>❶
    </div>
    <form method="post">❷
        <ul class="rounded">
            <li><input type="text" placeholder="Food" name="food" id="food"
                autocapitalize="off" autocorrect="off"
                autocomplete="off" /></li>
            <li><input type="text" placeholder="Calories" name="calories"
                id="calories" autocapitalize="off" autocorrect="off"
                autocomplete="off" /></li>
            <li><input type="submit" class="submit" name="action"
                value="Save Entry" /></li>❸
        </ul>
    </form>
</div>
```

❶ The first thing to point out about the New Entry panel is that rather than having a Back button, it has a Cancel button.

> Cancel buttons in jQTouch behave just like back buttons: they remove the current page from view with the reverse animation that it came into view. However, cancel buttons are not shaped like a left arrow as back buttons are.
>
> I used a Cancel button here for the New Entry panel because it slides up on the way in, and will therefore slide down on the way out. It would be counterintuitive to click a left-pointing Back button and then have the panel slide down.

❷ This HTML form contains an unordered (bulleted) list of three items: two text fields and a submit button. Embedding form controls in an `li` allows the `jqt` theme to style the form as shown in Figure 4-6.

Each of the text inputs has quite a few attributes defined:

`type="text"`
: Defines the form control to be a single line text entry field.

`placeholder`
: A string of text to display in the form input when the input is empty.

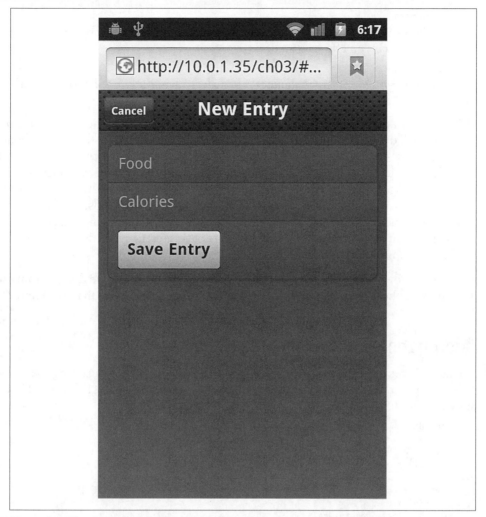

Figure 4-6. The jqt theme does a nice job styling form elements

name

> The name that will be associated with the value provided by the user when the form is submitted.

id

> A unique identifier for the element in the context of the entire page.

autocapitalize

> Allows you to control the autocapitalization feature in Mobile Safari on the iPhone. Has no effect on Android.

autocorrect

Allows you to control the spelling correction feature in Mobile Safari on the iPhone. Has no effect on Android.

autocomplete

Allows you to control the autocomplete feature in Mobile Safari on the iPhone. Has no effect on Android.

❸ The class attribute of the submit input button needs explanation. The Android phone will display a keyboard whenever the user's cursor is in a field. The keyboard has a Go button in the bottom right-hand corner that submits the form when clicked. When you are hijacking the submit function as we are doing here, submitting from the Go button on the keyboard does not remove the cursor from the active field and therefore, the keyboard does not slide out of view. To remedy this, jQTouch offers a convenience method that automatically removes the cursor from the active field when a form is submitted. To take advantage of this feature, add the submit class to the submit element of the form.

Figure 4-7 shows the New Entry form in action. At this point, we've done nothing to actually save the entry when the user clicks Save Entry. We'll cover that in Chapter 5.

Adding the Settings Panel

We haven't yet created a button that will allow users to navigate to a Settings panel, so let's add one to the toolbar on the Home panel. All it takes is a single line of HTML, shown in bold:

```
  </head>
  <body>
    <div id="home">
      <div class="toolbar">
          <h1>Kilo</h1>
          <a class="button flip" href="#settings">Settings</a>❶
      </div>
      <ul class="edgetoedge">
          <li class="arrow"><a href="#dates">Dates</a></li>
          <li class="arrow"><a href="#about">About</a></li>
      </ul>
    </div>
  ... remaining HTML not shown ...
```

❶ This is the line of HTML that adds the button (Figure 4-8). Notice that we've assigned the flip class to the link. The flip class instructs jQTouch to transition from the Home panel to the Settings panel by rotating the page on its vertical axis. To give an added dimension to the process, the page actually zooms out a bit during the animation. Fancy, no?

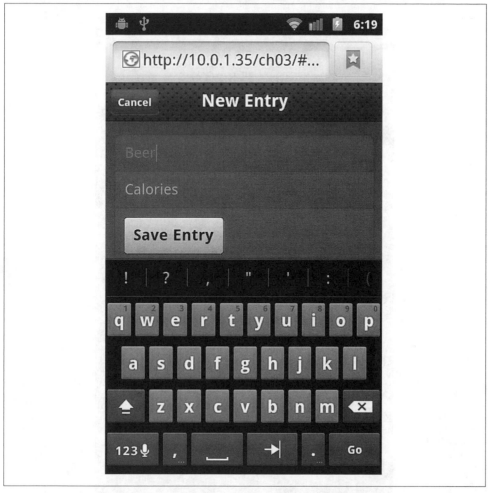

Figure 4-7. Keyboard data entry with the New Entry form

 Unfortunately, support for 3D animations is spotty across mobile platforms, including Android. Therefore flip, swap, cube, and any other 3D animations will failover to 2D animations when 3D is not supported.

After working on the New Entry panel, the HTML for the Settings panel is going to look pretty similar (Example 4-6). There is one more text input and some of the attributes have been omitted or have different values, but conceptually they are identical. Add this to your HTML document just as you've done with the HTML for the other panels.

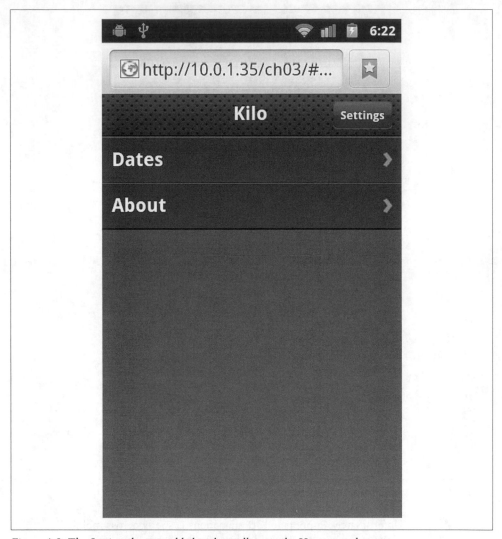

Figure 4-8. The Settings button added to the toolbar on the Home panel

As with the New Entry form, the Settings form does not currently save any of the information associated with it (see Figure 4-9). Its submission handler will be described in the next chapter.

Example 4-6. The HTML for the Settings panel

```
<div id="settings">
    <div class="toolbar">
        <h1>Settings</h1>
        <a class="button cancel" href="#">Cancel</a>
    </div>
```

```
<form method="post">
    <ul class="rounded">
        <li><input placeholder="Age" type="text" name="age" id="age" /></li>
        <li><input placeholder="Weight" type="text"
                name="weight" id="weight" /></li>
        <li><input placeholder="Budget" type="text"
                name="budgct" id="budget" /></li>
        <li><input type="submit" class="submit" name="action"
            value="Save Changes" /></li>
    </ul>
</form>
</div>
```

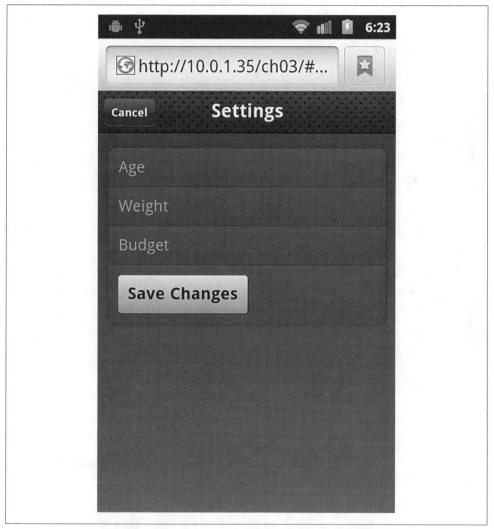

Figure 4-9. The Settings panel

Putting It All Together

So, there you have it. With fewer than 100 lines of code, we've created a native-style UI for a five-panel application complete with three different page transition animations. See Example 4-7 for a complete listing of the final HTML. Not too shabby, right?

Example 4-7. The complete HTML listing for the five-panel UI

```
<html>
    <head>
        <title>Kilo</title>
        <link type="text/css" rel="stylesheet" media="screen"
            href="jqtouch/jqtouch.css">
        <link type="text/css" rel="stylesheet" media="screen"
            href="themes/jqt/theme.css">
        <script type="text/javascript" src="jqtouch/jquery.js"></script>
        <script type="text/javascript" src="jqtouch/jqtouch.js"></script>
        <script type="text/javascript">
            var jQT = $.jQTouch({
                icon: 'kilo.png'
            });
        </script>
    </head>
    <body>
        <div id="home">
            <div class="toolbar">
                <h1>Kilo</h1>
                <a class="button flip" href="#settings">Settings</a>
            </div>
            <ul class="edgetoedge">
                <li class="arrow"><a href="#dates">Dates</a></li>
                <li class="arrow"><a href="#about">About</a></li>
            </ul>
        </div>
        <div id="about">
            <div class="toolbar">
                <h1>About</h1>
                <a class="button back" href="#">Back</a>
            </div>
            <div>
                <p>Kilo gives you easy access to your food diary.</p>
            </div>
        </div>
        <div id="dates">
            <div class="toolbar">
                <h1>Dates</h1>
                <a class="button back" href="#">Back</a>
            </div>
            <ul class="edgetoedge">
                <li class="arrow"><a id="0" href="#date">Today</a></li>
                <li class="arrow"><a id="1" href="#date">Yesterday</a></li>
                <li class="arrow"><a id="2" href="#date">2 Days Ago</a></li>
                <li class="arrow"><a id="3" href="#date">3 Days Ago</a></li>
```

```
                <li class="arrow"><a id="4" href="#date">4 Days Ago</a></li>
                <li class="arrow"><a id="5" href="#date">5 Days Ago</a></li>
            </ul>
        </div>
        <div id="date">
            <div class="toolbar">
                <h1>Date</h1>
                <a class="button back" href="#">Back</a>
                <a class="button slideup" href="#createEntry">+</a>
            </div>
            <ul class="edgetoedge">
                <li id="entryTemplate" class="entry" style="display:none">
                    <span class="label">Label</span>
                    <span class="calories">000</span>
                    <span class="delete">Delete</span>
                </li>
            </ul>
        </div>
        <div id="createEntry">
            <div class="toolbar">
                <h1>New Entry</h1>
                <a class="button cancel" href="#">Cancel</a>
            </div>
            <form method="post">
                <ul class="rounded">
                    <li><input type="text" placeholder="Food" name="food" id="food"
                        autocapitalize="off" autocorrect="off"
                        autocomplete="off" /></li>
                    <li><input type="text" placeholder="Calories" name="calories"
                        id="calories" autocapitalize="off" autocorrect="off"
                        autocomplete="off" /></li>
                    <li><input type="submit" class="submit" name="action"
                        value="Save Entry" /></li>
                </ul>
            </form>
        </div>
        <div id="settings">
            <div class="toolbar">
                <h1>Settings</h1>
                <a class="button cancel" href="#">Cancel</a>
            </div>
            <form method="post">
                <ul class="rounded">
                    <li><input placeholder="Age" type="text" name="age" id="age" /></li>
                    <li><input placeholder="Weight" type="text"
                        name="weight" id="weight" /></li>
                    <li><input placeholder="Budget" type="text"
                        name="budget" id="budget" /></li>
                    <li><input type="submit" class="submit" name="action"
                        value="Save Changes" /></li>
                </ul>
            </form>
        </div>
    </body>
</html>
```

Customizing jQTouch

You can customize the jQTouch default behavior by sending a variety of property settings into the constructor. You saw this previously with the icon property, but there are several others that you should be aware of, shown in Table 4-1.

Table 4-1. jQTouch customization options

Property	Default	Expects	Notes
addGlossToIcon	true	true or false	If set to true, gloss will be added to the home screen icon on iPhone. Has no effect on Android.
backSelector	'.back, .cancel, .goback'	Any valid CSS selector; separate multiple values with a comma	Defines elements that will trigger the "back" behavior of jQTouch when tapped. When the back behavior is invoked, the current panel moves off screen with a reverse animation and is removed from history.
cacheGetRequests	true	true or false	If set to true, automatically caches GET requests, so subsequent clicks reference the already-loaded data.
cubeSelector	'.cube'	Any valid CSS selector; separate multiple values with a comma	Defines elements that will trigger a cube animation from the current panel to the target panel.
dissolveSelector	'.dissolve'	Any valid CSS selector; separate multiple values with a comma	Defines elements that will trigger a dissolve animation from the current panel to the target panel.
fadeSelector	'.fade'	Any valid CSS selector; separate multiple values with a comma	Defines elements that will trigger a fade animation from the current panel to the target panel.
fixedViewport	true	true or false	If set to true, prevents users from being able to zoom in or out of the page.
flipSelector	'.flip'	Any valid CSS selector; separate multiple values with a comma	Defines elements that will trigger a flip animation from the current panel to the target panel.
formSelector	'form'	Any valid CSS selector; separate multiple values with a comma	Defines elements that should receive the onsubmit handler.
fullScreen	true	true or false	iPhone only; has no effect on Android. When set to true, your app will open in full-screen mode when launched from the user's home screen. Has no effect on the display if the app is running in Mobile Safari.

Property	Default	Expects	Notes
fullScreenClass	'fullscreen'	String	iPhone only; has no effect on Android. Class name that will be applied to the body when the app is launched in full-screen mode. Allows you to write custom CSS that only executes in full-screen mode.
icon	null	null or a relative or absolute path to a *.png* image file	The home screen icon for your app. This is the image that will be displayed when a user adds a bookmark for your app to his home screen.
popSelector	'.pop'	Any valid CSS selector; separate multiple values with a comma	Defines elements that will trigger a pop animation from the current panel to the target panel.
preloadImages	false	An array of image paths	Defines images that will be loaded before the page loads. For example: ['images/link_over.png', 'images/link_select.png']
slideInSelector	'ul li a'	Any valid CSS selector; separate multiple values with a comma	Defines elements that will trigger a slide left animation from the current panel to the target panel.
slideupSelector	'.slideup'	Any valid CSS selector; separate multiple values with a comma	Defines elements that will cause the target panel to slide up into view in front of the current panel.
startupScreen	null	null or a relative or absolute path to an image file	iPhone only; has no effect on Android. Pass a relative or absolute path to a 320px × 460px startup screen for full-screen apps. Use a 320px × 480px image if you set statusBar to black-translucent.
statusBar	'default'	default, black-translucent, black	iPhone only; has no effect on Android. Defines the appearance of the 20-pixel status bar at the top of the window in an app launched in full-screen mode.
submitSelector	'.submit'	Any valid CSS selector; separate multiple values with a comma	Selector that, when clicked, will submit its parent form (and close keyboard If open).
swapSelector	'.swap'	Any valid CSS selector; separate multiple values with a comma	Defines elements that will cause the target panel to swap into view in front of the current panel.
useAnimations	true	true or false	Set to false to disable all animations.

What You've Learned

In this chapter, you've learned how to add native-looking animations to a web app using jQTouch. In the next chapter, you'll learn how to use the new local storage and client-side database features of HTML5 to add persistent data storage to your app.

CHAPTER 5

Client-Side Data Storage

Most software applications need to store data in some sort of persistent fashion in order to be useful. When it comes to web apps, this task has traditionally been handled with either a server-side database or cookies set in the browser. With the advent of HTML5, web developers now have a couple more options: Web Storage, and Web SQL Database.

Web Storage

Web Storage comes in two flavors—`localStorage` and `sessionStorage`—and are very similar to cookies in that they allow you to use JavaScript to set name/value pairs that you can retrieve across multiple page reloads.

Unlike cookies, however, Web Storage data is not sent across the wire with the browser request—it lives entirely in the client. Therefore, it's feasible to store much more data than you can with cookies.

 At the time of this writing, browser size limits for Web Storage are still in flux. However, my most recent tests indicate that the limit is right around 2.5 MB.

Functionally, `localStorage` and `sessionStorage` are the same. They differ only in terms of persistence and scope:

`localStorage`
> Data is saved even after the window is closed and is available to all windows (or tabs) that are loaded from the same origin (must be the same domain name, protocol, and port). This is useful for things like application preferences.

sessionStorage

Data is stored with the window object. Other windows/tabs are not aware of the values, and the data is discarded when the window/tab is closed. Useful for window-specific state like active tab highlight or the sort order of a table.

 In any of the following examples, you can substitute sessionStorage anywhere you see localStorage, but remember that sessionStorage goes away when you close the window or tab.

Setting a value is as simple as the following:

```
localStorage.setItem('age', 40);
```

Accessing a stored value is equally simple:

```
var age = localStorage.getItem('age');
```

You can delete a specific key/value pair from storage like so:

```
localStorage.removeItem('age');
```

Or, you can delete all key/value pairs like so:

```
localStorage.clear();
```

Assuming your keys are valid JavaScript tokens (e.g., no spaces, no punctuation other than underscores) you can use this alternate syntax:

```
localStorage.age = 40 // Set the value of age
var age = localStorage.age; // Get the value of age
delete localStorage.age; // Remove age from storage
```

 The localStorage and sessionStorage keys are stored separately. If you use the same key name for each, they will not conflict with each other.

Saving User Settings to Local Storage

On to a practical example. Let's update the Settings panel of the example app you started working on in Chapter 4 so that it stores the form values in localStorage.

We are going to be writing a fair amount of JavaScript in this chapter, and I don't want to jam it all in the head section of our HTML document. To keep our code organized, create a file called *kilo.js* in the same directory as your HTML document, and update the head of your HTML document with a reference to *kilo.js*:

```
<head>
    <title>Kilo</title>
    <link type="text/css" rel="stylesheet" media="screen"
        href="jqtouch/jqtouch.css">
```

```
<link type="text/css" rel="stylesheet" media="screen"
    href="themes/jqt/theme.css">
<script type="text/javascript" src="jqtouch/jquery.js"></script>
<script type="text/javascript" src="jqtouch/jqtouch.js"></script>
<script type="text/javascript" src="kilo.js"></script>
</head>
```

Alert readers will notice that I've also removed the jQTouch constructor from the head of the HTML document. It's not gone, though; I just moved it into *kilo.js*. Be sure you remove that from your main HTML file and create the *kilo.js* file in the same directory with the following contents, then reload the main HTML document in your browser to make sure it's still working:

```
var jQT = $.jQTouch({
    icon: 'kilo.png'
});
```

With that little bit of code reorganization out of the way, it's time to add the code needed to save the settings. You need to override the submit action of the Settings form and replace it with a custom function called saveSettings(). Thanks to jQuery, you can accomplish this with a single line of code, which you must place in the document ready function. Add the following to *kilo.js*:

```
$(document).ready(function(){
    $('#settings form').submit(saveSettings);
});
```

The net result of this is that when the user submits the settings form, the save Settings() function will run instead of the form actually getting submitted.

When the saveSettings() function is called, it grabs the values from the three form inputs using jQuery's val() function and saves each in a localStorage variable of the same name. Add this function to *kilo.js*:

```
function saveSettings() {
    localStorage.age = $('#age').val();
    localStorage.budget = $('#budget').val();
    localStorage.weight = $('#weight').val();
    jQT.goBack();
    return false;
}
```

Once the values are stored, this function uses the jQuery goBack() function (on the second-to-last line) to dismiss the panel and return to the previous page. Next, it returns false to prevent the default action of the submit event that triggers this function. Had we omitted this line, the current page would reload, which is not what we want.

At this point, a user can launch the app, navigate to the Settings panel, enter her settings, and submit the form to save the settings to localStorage.

Since we are not clearing the fields when the form is submitted, the values that the user enters will still be there when she navigates back to the Settings panel. However, this is not because the values have been saved to `localStorage`; it's because they are still sitting there after having been typed in.

Therefore, the next time the user launches that app and navigates to the Settings panel, the fields will be empty, even though they have been saved.

To remedy this, we need to load the settings using the `loadSettings()` function, so add the following function to *kilo.js*:

```
function loadSettings() {
    $('#age').val(localStorage.age);
    $('#budget').val(localStorage.budget);
    $('#weight').val(localStorage.weight);
}
```

The `loadSettings()` function is the opposite of the `saveSettings()` function; it uses jQuery's `val()` function to set the three fields of the Settings form to the corresponding values saved in `localStorage`.

Now that we have a `loadSettings()` function, we need to trigger it. The most obvious time to do this is when the app launches. To make this happen, simply add a line to the `document ready` function in *kilo.js*:

```
$(document).ready(function(){
    $('#settings form').submit(saveSettings);
    loadSettings();
});
```

Unfortunately, loading the settings only at startup leaves a loophole that occurs if the user navigates to the Settings panel, changes some values, and taps the Cancel button without submitting the form.

In this case, the newly changed values will still be sitting there the next time the user visits the Settings panel; not because the values were saved (they weren't), but because they are still just sitting there. If the user closes and reopens the app, the displayed values will revert to the saved values because the `loadSettings()` function will refresh them at startup.

There are several ways to rectify this situation, but I think the most appropriate is to refresh the displayed values whenever the Settings panel begins to move, either into or out of view.

Thanks to jQTouch, this is a simple matter of binding the `loadSettings()` function to the `pageAnimationStart` event of the Settings panel. Replace the line you just added with the code shown in bold:

```
$(document).ready(function(){
    $('#settings form').submit(saveSettings);
    $('#settings').bind('pageAnimationStart', loadSettings);
});
```

This leaves one little problem: if the local storage variables have never been defined, loadSettings() won't replace the form variables. So you need to add these lines of code to the top of loadSettings(), which sets the local storage variables to blank values if they aren't defined:

```
if (!localStorage.age) {
    localStorage.age - "";
}
if (!localStorage.budget) {
    localStorage.budget = "";
}
if (!localStorage.weight) {
    localStorage.weight = "";
}
```

The JavaScript contained in the *kilo.js* file now provides persistent data support for the Settings panel. When you view the code we've written to make this happen, there's really not much to it. Here is everything in *kilo.js* so far:

```
var jQT = $.jQTouch({
    icon: 'kilo.png'
});
$(document).ready(function(){
    $('#settings form').submit(saveSettings);
    $('#settings').bind('pageAnimationStart', loadSettings);
});
function saveSettings() {
    localStorage.age = $('#age').val();
    localStorage.budget = $('#budget').val();
    localStorage.weight = $('#weight').val();
    jQT.goBack();
    return false;
}
function loadSettings() {
    if (!localStorage.age) {
        localStorage.age = "";
    }
    if (!localStorage.budget) {
        localStorage.budget = "";
    }
    if (!localStorage.weight) {
        localStorage.weight = "";
    }
    $('#age').val(localStorage.age);
    $('#budget').val(localStorage.budget);
    $('#weight').val(localStorage.weight);
}
```

Saving the Selected Date to Session Storage

Ultimately, what we want to do is set up the Date panel so that when it's displayed, it will check the database for any records entered for that date and display them as an edge-to-edge list. This requires that the Date panel know which date the user tapped on the Dates panel.

We also want to allow the user to add and delete entries from the database, so we'll have to add support for the + button that already exists on the Date panel, and for the Delete button in the Date panel entry template (more on this later).

The first step is to let the Date panel know which item the user clicked when she navigated to it from the Dates panel. With this piece of information, you can calculate the appropriate date context. To do so, you need to add some lines to the document ready function in *kilo.js*:

```
$(document).ready(function(){
    $('#settings form').submit(saveSettings);
    $('#settings').bind('pageAnimationStart', loadSettings);
    $('#dates li a').bind('click touchend', function(){❶
        var dayOffset = this.id;❷
        var date = new Date();❸
        date.setDate(date.getDate() - dayOffset);
        sessionStorage.currentDate = date.getMonth() + 1 + '/' +
                                     date.getDate() + '/' +
                                     date.getFullYear();❹
        refreshEntries();❺
    });
});
```

❶ On this line, jQuery's bind() function attaches the JavaScript code that follows to the click and touchend events of the links on the Dates panel. We are binding to the touchend event to achieve the optimal experience on the phone, and binding to the click event so we can continue testing in a desktop browser (which doesn't support the touchend event).

❷ This line of code grabs the ID of the clicked object and stores it in the dayOffset variable. As you may recall, the links on the Dates panel have IDs ranging from 0 to 5, so the ID of the clicked link will correspond to the number of days needed to calculate the clicked date (i.e., 0 days in the past equals today, 1 day in the past equals yesterday, 2 days in the past equals the day before yesterday).

 In this context, the this keyword will contain a reference to the object that was the target of the click event.

❸ This line creates a new JavaScript Date object and stores it in a variable named date. Initially, this date will be set to the particular moment in time that it was created, so on the next line, we subtract the dayOffset from the result of the getDate() function and use setDate() to change the date to the selected date (a dayOffset of 0 would be today, 1 would be yesterday, and so on).

❹ This code builds a MM/DD/YYYY–formatted date string and saves it to session Storage as currentDate.

 The getMonth() method of the Date object returns values from 0–11, January being 0. Therefore, we have to add 1 to generate the correct value for the formatted string.

❺ Finally, we call the refreshEntries() function. The job of the refreshEntries() function is to update the incoming Date panel appropriately based on the date the user tapped on the Dates panel. For now, we'll just set it to update the toolbar title of the Dates panel with the selected date so you can see it's working. Without it, you'd just see the word "Date," as shown in Figure 5-1. Figure 5-2 shows the refreshEntries() function in action. Add the following function to *kilo.js*:

```
function refreshEntries() {
    var currentDate = sessionStorage.currentDate;
    $('#date h1').text(currentDate);
}
```

Next, we'll move on to a more powerful and complex client-side data storage method that we'll use to store the user's food entries on the Date panel.

Web SQL Database

Of all the exciting features of HTML5, the one that rocks my world the most is the Web SQL Database. The Web SQL Database spec gives developers a simple but powerful JavaScript database API to store persistent data in a local SQLite database.

 Technically, the Web SQL Database spec is not part of HTML5. It was broken out of the original HTML5 spec into its own spec, but in casual conversation, it's often still referred to as an "HTML5 feature."

Developers can use standard SQL statements to create tables and to insert, update, select, and delete rows. The JavaScript database API even supports transactions. We're talking about SQL here, so there is an inherent complexity. Regardless, this is a game-changing feature, so you will be well rewarded if you spend time getting your head around it.

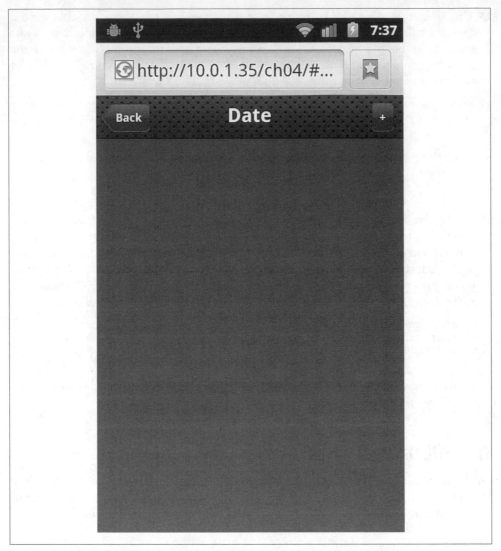

Figure 5-1. Before the refreshEntries() function, the title just says "Date"...

Creating a Database

Now that our Date panel knows which date the user has selected, we have all the information we need to allow the user to create entries. Before we can write the createEntry() function, we need to set up a database table to store the submitted data (this is a one-time operation). We'll add some lines to *kilo.js* to do so:

```
var db; ❶
$(document).ready(function(){
    $('#settings form').submit(saveSettings);
    $('#settings').bind('pageAnimationStart', loadSettings);
```

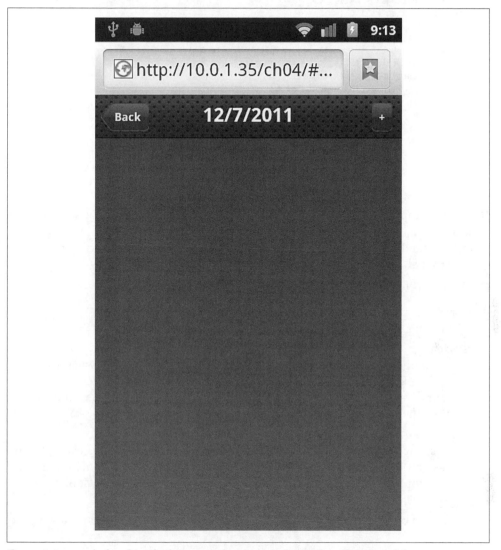

Figure 5-2. …and after the refreshEntries() function, the title reflects the selected date

```
$('#dates li a').bind('click touchend', function(){
    var dayOffset = this.id;
    var date = new Date();
    date.setDate(date.getDate() - dayOffset);
    sessionStorage.currentDate = date.getMonth() + 1 + '/' +
                                 date.getDate() + '/' +
                                 date.getFullYear();
    refreshEntries();
});
```

```
        var shortName = 'Kilo';❷
        var version = '1.0';
        var displayName = 'Kilo';
        var maxSize = 65536;
        db = openDatabase(shortName, version, displayName, maxSize);❸
        db.transaction(❹
            function(transaction) {❺
                transaction.executeSql(❻
                    'CREATE TABLE IF NOT EXISTS entries ' +
                    '  (id INTEGER NOT NULL PRIMARY KEY AUTOINCREMENT, ' +
                    '   date DATE NOT NULL, food TEXT NOT NULL, ' +
                    ' calories INTEGER NOT NULL );'
                );
            }
        );
    });
```

❶ The first thing to note is there is a variable named db in the global scope of the application. This variable is to hold a reference to the database connection once we've established it. It is defined in the global scope because we're going to have to refer to it all over the place.

❷ These four lines define some vars for the openDatabase call:

shortName
: A string that will refer to the database file on disk.

version
: A number for managing upgrades and backward compatibility when you need to change your database schema (i.e., check the database version on app launch—if it's old, create the new database and migrate the data from one to the other, as shown in "Geolocation" on page 133).

displayName
: A string that will be presented in the interface to the user. For example, the display name appears in the Storage tab of the Developer Tools in Chrome desktop (Click the wrench icon, then choose Tools→Developer Tools).

maxSize
: The maximum number of kilobytes to which you will allow your database to grow.

Database size limits are still being implemented by browser vendors at this time, but the W3C recommends an arbitrary 5 MB limit per origin. If your database grows beyond the limit, the user will automatically be asked to allow or deny the size increase. If he allows the increase, the database size limit will be upped to 10 MB. If he denies the increase, a QUOTA_ERR error will be returned. See Table 5-1 for a list of database error codes.

❸ With the parameters set, this line calls `openDatabase` and stores the connection in the `db` variable. If the database doesn't already exist, it will be created.

❹ All database queries must take place in the context of a transaction, so we begin one here by calling the `transaction` method of the `db` object. The remaining lines make up a function that is sent to the transaction as the sole parameter.

❺ This line begins an anonymous function and passes the transaction object into it. To be perfectly honest, I think passing the transaction object into its own callback function is weird (why not just use `this`?), but that's what you have to do.

❻ Once inside the function, we call the `executeSql` method of the transaction object to execute a standard `CREATE TABLE` query. The `IF NOT EXISTS` clause prevents the table from being created if it already exists.

If you were to launch the app as is, it would create a database named Kilo on the Android phone.

In the desktop version of Chrome, you can actually view and interact with your client-side databases by clicking the wrench icon then choosing Tools→Developer Tools, and clicking the Resources tab and looking for Databases, Local Storage, and Session Storage on the left side of the screen.

The Developer Tools included in desktop Chrome are extremely helpful when debugging. By default, it appears as a pane of your current browser window. If you click the undock icon (hover over the icons at the bottom left to see what they do), it will appear in a separate window, as shown in Figure 5-3. The interface even allows you to send arbitrary SQL queries to the database by clicking on the database name (see Figure 5-4).

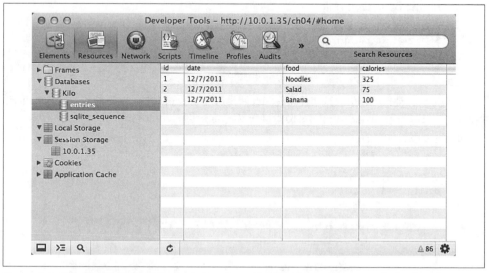

Figure 5-3. The Storage tab in Chrome's Developer Tools with some test records displayed

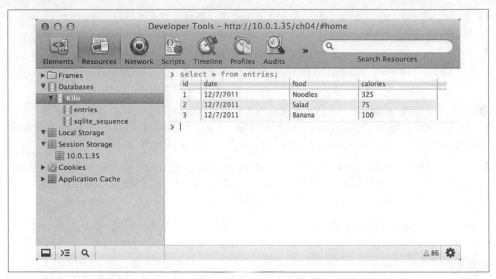

Figure 5-4. The Storage tab in Chrome's Developer Tools allows you to execute arbitrary SQL statements against your database

Inserting Rows

Now that we have a database set up to receive some entries, we can set about building the createEntry() function. First, you have to override the submit event of the #createEntry form. You can do so by binding the createEntry() function to the submit event in the document ready function in *kilo.js* (here I just show the first few lines with the added line of code in bold):

```
$(document).ready(function(){
    $('#createEntry form').submit(createEntry);
    $('#settings form').submit(saveSettings);
    $('#settings').bind('pageAnimationStart', loadSettings);
    ...
```

Now when a user submits the #createEntry form, the createEntry() function is called. Next, add the following to *kilo.js* to create the record in the database:

```
function createEntry() {
    var date = sessionStorage.currentDate;❶
    var calories = $('#calories').val();
    var food = $('#food').val();
    db.transaction(❷
        function(transaction) {
            transaction.executeSql(
                'INSERT INTO entries (date, calories, food) VALUES (?, ?, ?);',
                [date, calories, food],
                function(){
                    refreshEntries();
                    jQT.goBack();
```

```
            },
            errorHandler
        );
    }
);
return false;
}
```

❶ This section contains some variables that we're going to use in the SQL query. As you may recall (from "Saving the Selected Date to Session Storage" on page 84), the date the user taps on the Dates panel is stored in `sessionStorage.currentDate`. The other two values (calories and food) are pulled out of the data entry form using the same approach that we used earlier with the Settings form.

❷ This code opens a database transaction and runs an `executeSql()` call. Here we are passing four parameters to the `executeSql()` method:

`'INSERT INTO entries (date, calories, food) VALUES (?, ?, ?);'`
> This is the statement that will be executed. The question marks are data placeholders.

`[date, calories, food]`
> This is an array of the values being sent to the database. They correspond by position with the data placeholder question marks in the SQL statement.

`function(){refreshEntries();jQT.goBack();}`
> This anonymous function will execute if the SQL query is successful.

`errorHandler`
> This is the name of the function that will execute if the SQL query fails.

Quotes (' or ") around the ? placeholders are not necessary—escaping and quoting of data is handled automatically.

Error handling

Assuming the insert is successful, the anonymous function passed as the third parameter will be executed. It calls the `refreshEntries()` function (at the moment, this function only updates the title of the Date panel, but soon it will make entries you create appear in the list there) and it simulates a tap on the Cancel button to dismiss the New Entry panel and return to the Date panel. As we saw earlier with the Settings panel, the Cancel button does not cancel the submit action—it's really just a Back button labeled "Cancel" that isn't shaped like a left arrow.

If the insert is not successful, the errorHandler() function will run. Add the following to the *kilo.js* file:

```
function errorHandler(transaction, error) {
    alert('Oops. Error was '+error.message+' (Code '+error.code+')');
    return true;
}
```

The error handler is passed two parameters: the transaction object and the error object. Here, we're using the error object to alert the user to the message and error code that were thrown.

Error handlers must return true or false. When an error handler returns true (i.e., "Yes, this is a fatal error"), execution is halted and the entire transaction is rolled back. When an error handler returns false (i.e., "No, this is not a fatal error"), execution will continue.

In some cases, you might want to branch based on the type of error to decide whether you should return true or false. Table 5-1, at the end of this chapter, shows the (current) possible error codes according to the W3C Web SQL Database working draft specification.

Executing SQL Inside the Error Handler

You may have noticed that the error handler function accepts a transaction object in addition to the error object. It's conceivable that in some cases you might want to execute a SQL statement inside the error handler, perhaps to log the error or record some metadata for debugging or crash-reporting purposes. The transaction object parameter allows you to make more executeSql() calls from inside the error handler, like so (this is just an example; it will not run unless you've created the errors table that it refers to):

```
function errorHandler(transaction, error) {
    alert('Oops. Error was '+error.message+' (Code '+error.code+')');
    transaction.executeSql('INSERT INTO errors (code, message) VALUES (?, ?);',
                            [error.code, error.message]);
    return false;
}
```

Please take special note of the fact that we have to return false from the error handler if we want the executeSql() statement to run. If we return true (or nothing at all), the entire transaction—including this SQL statement—will be rolled back, thereby preventing the desired result.

Although I won't be doing so in my examples, you should know that you can also specify success and error handlers on the `transaction` method itself. This gives you a convenient location to execute code after a long series of `executeSql()` statements have completed.

Oddly, the parameter order for the `transaction` method's callbacks is defined to be error, then success (the reverse of the order for `executeSql()`). Here's a version of the `createEntry()` function with transaction callbacks added toward the end (don't add these to *kilo.js*, because we haven't defined either of these methods):

```
function createEntry() {
    var date = sessionStorage.currentDate;
    var calories = $('#calories').val();
    var food = $('#food').val();
    db.transaction(
        function(transaction) {
            transaction.executeSql(
                'INSERT INTO entries (date, calories, food) VALUES (?, ?, ?);',
                [date, calories, food],
                function(){
                    refreshEntries();
                    jQT.goBack();
                },
                errorHandler
            );
        },
        transactionErrorHandler,
        transactionSuccessHandler
    );
    return false;
}
```

Selecting Rows and Handling Result Sets

The next step is to expand the `refreshEntries()` function to do more than just set the title bar to the selected date. Specifically, we'll query the database for entries on the selected date and append them to the `#date ul` element using the hidden `entryTemplate` HTML for structure. It's been a while since we looked at that code, so here's the Date panel again (it's already in *index.html*, so you don't need to add it again):

```
<div id="date">
    <div class="toolbar">
        <h1>Date</h1>
        <a class="button back" href="#">Back</a>
        <a class="button slideup" href="#createEntry">+</a>
    </div>
    <ul class="edgetoedge">
        <li id="entryTemplate" class="entry" style="display:none">❶
            <span class="label">Label</span>
            <span class="calories">000</span>
            <span class="delete">Delete</span>
        </li>
    </ul>
</div>
```

❶ Recall that we had set the style attribute of the li to `display: none`, which makes it not show up on the page. We did this so we could use that HTML snippet as a template for the database rows.

Here's the complete `refreshEntries()` function; you must replace the existing `refreshEntries()` function in *kilo.js* with this:

```
function refreshEntries() {
    var currentDate = sessionStorage.currentDate;❶
    $('#date h1').text(currentDate);
    $('#date ul li:gt(0)').remove();❷
    db.transaction(❸
        function(transaction) {
            transaction.executeSql(
                'SELECT * FROM entries WHERE date = ? ORDER BY food;',❹
                [currentDate], ❺
                function (transaction, result) {❻
                    for (var i=0; i < result.rows.length; i++) {
                        var row = result.rows.item(i);❼
                        var newEntryRow = $('#entryTemplate').clone();❽
                        newEntryRow.removeAttr('id');
                        newEntryRow.removeAttr('style');
                        newEntryRow.data('entryId', row.id);❾
                        newEntryRow.appendTo('#date ul');❿
                        newEntryRow.find('.label').text(row.food);
                        newEntryRow.find('.calories').text(row.calories);
                    }
                },
                errorHandler
            );
        }
    );
}
```

❶ These two lines set the toolbar title of the Date panel to the contents of the `current Date` value saved in `sessionStorage`.

❷ This line uses jQuery's `gt()` function (gt stands for "greater than") to select and remove any li elements with an index greater than 0. The first time through, this will do nothing because the only li will be the one with the ID of `entryTemplate`, which has an index of 0 and is hidden anyhow. However, on subsequent visits to the page, we need to remove any other lis before appending rows from the database again. Otherwise, items would end up appearing multiple times in the list because we'd be adding the same items over and over again.

❸ These three lines set up a database transaction and the `executeSql` statement.

❹ This line contains the first parameter for the `executeSql` statement. It's a simple `SELECT` statement with a question mark acting as a data placeholder.

❺ This is a single-element array that contains the currently selected date. This will replace the question mark in the SQL query.

❻ This anonymous function will be called in the event of a successful query. It accepts two parameters: `transaction` and `result`.

The `transaction` object can be used within the success handler to send new queries to the database, as we saw with the error handler previously. However, there is no need to do that in this case, so we won't be using it.

The `result` object is what we are most interested in here. It has three read-only properties: `rowsAffected`, which you can use to determine the number of rows affected by an insert, update, or delete query; `insertId`, which returns the primary key of the last row created in an insert operation; and `rows`, which has the records that were found.

The `rows` object will contain 0 or more `row` objects and has a `length` property that appears in the `for` loop on the next line.

❼ This line uses the `item()` method of the `rows` object to set the `row` variable to the contents of the current row.

❽ On this line, we `clone()` the template `li` and remove its `id` and `style` attributes on the next two lines. Removing the style will make the row visible, and removing the `id` is important because otherwise we would end up with multiple items on the page with the same `id`.

❾ This line stores the value of the `row`'s `id` property as data on the `li` itself (we'll need that later in case the user decides to delete the entry).

❿ This code appends the `li` element to the parent `ul`. The next two lines update the `label` and `calories` span child elements of the `li` with the corresponding data from the `row` object.

With all this out of the way, our Date panel will display an `li` for each row in the database that corresponds to the selected date. Each row will have a label, calories, and a Delete button. Once we create a few rows, you can see that we need to add a bit of CSS to style things up nicely (Figure 5-5).

Save the following CSS into a file named *kilo.css* (save this in the same directory as the HTML file):

```css
#date ul li {
    position: relative;
}
#date ul li span {
    color: #FFFFFF;
    text-shadow: 0 1px 2px rgba(0,0,0,.7);
}
#date ul li .delete {
    position: absolute;
    top: 5px;
    right: 6px;
    font-size: 12px;
    line-height: 30px;
```

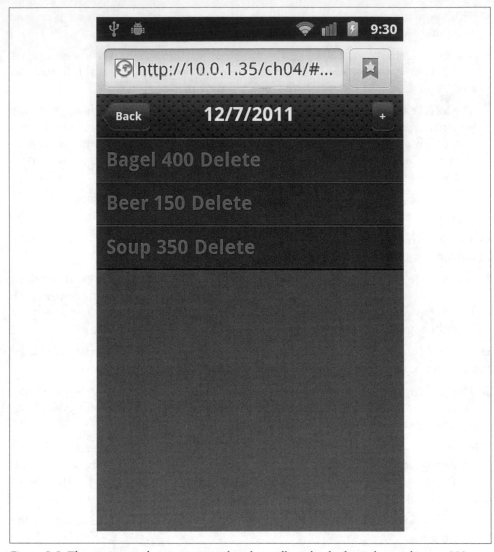

Figure 5-5. The entries are showing up now, but they still need to be fancied up with some CSS

```
    padding: 0 3px;
    border-width: 0 5px;
    -webkit-border-image: url(themes/jqt/img/button.png) 0 5 0 5;
}
```

Now, link to *kilo.css* by adding the following line to the head section of *index.html*:

```
<link type="text/css" rel="stylesheet" media="screen" href="kilo.css">
```

Although the Delete buttons now look like buttons (see Figure 5-6), they won't do anything when tapped at this point. This is because we set them up using the span tag, which is not an interactive element in an HTML page.

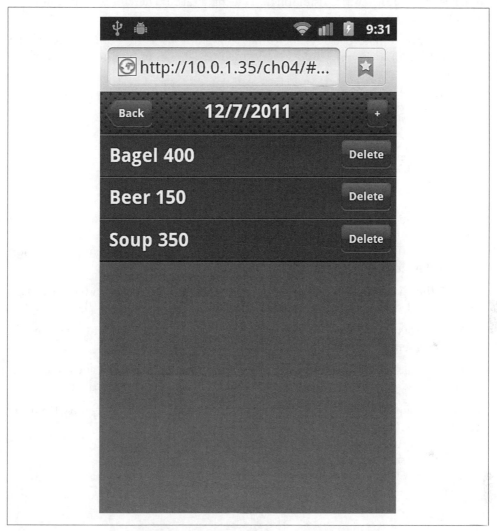

Figure 5-6. The entries with CSS applied

Deleting Rows

To make our Delete buttons do something when clicked, we need to bind a click event handler to them with jQuery.

Unfortunately, that approach won't work in this case. Unlike the items on the Dates panel, the entries on the Date panel are not static. This means they are added and removed throughout the course of the user's session. In fact, when the application launches, there are no entries visible on the Date panel at all. Therefore, we have nothing to bind the click to at launch.

The solution is to bind click events to the delete buttons as they are created by the refreshEntries() function. To do so, add the lines shown in bold to the end of the for loop:

```
    ...
    newEntryRow.find('.calories').text(row.calories);
    newEntryRow.find('.delete').click(function(){❶
        var clickedEntry = $(this).parent();❷
        var clickedEntryId = clickedEntry.data('entryId');❸
        deleteEntryById(clickedEntryId);❹
        clickedEntry.slideUp();
    });
}
```

❶ The function begins by specifying that we are looking for any elements that have a class of delete inside of an element that has an ID of date, and calls the click() method on those elements. The click() method accepts the anonymous function that will handle the event as its only parameter.

❷ When the click handler is triggered, the parent of the Delete button (i.e., the li) is located and stored in the clickedEntry variable.

❸ This line sets the clickedEntryId variable to the value of the entryId we stored on the li element when the refreshEntries() function created it.

❹ This line passes the clicked ID into the deleteEntryById() function, and on the next line, jQuery's slideUp() method gracefully removes the li from the page.

Add the following deleteEntryById() function to *kilo.js* to remove the entry from the database:

```
function deleteEntryById(id) {
    db.transaction(
        function(transaction) {
            transaction.executeSql('DELETE FROM entries WHERE id=?;',
              [id], null, errorHandler);
        }
    );
}
```

As we've done in previous examples, we open a transaction, pass it a callback function with the transaction object as the parameter, and call the executeSql() method. We're passing in the SQL query and the ID of the clicked record as the first two arguments. The third argument is where the success handler would go, but we don't need one, so we just specify null. As the fourth argument, we specify the same error handler that we've been using all along.

And there you have it. It may have taken a lot of description to get to this point, but in reality we haven't had to write all that much code. In fact, *kilo.js* only contains about 100 lines of JavaScript (Example 5-1).

Example 5-1. The complete JavaScript listing for Kilo database interaction

```javascript
var db;
var jQT = $.jQTouch({
    icon: 'kilo.png'
});
$(document).ready(function(){
    $('#createEntry form').submit(createEntry);
    $('#settings form').submit(saveSettings);
    $('#settings').bind('pageAnimationStart', loadSettings);
    $('#dates li a').bind('click touchend', function(){
        var dayOffset = this.id;
        var date = new Date();
        date.setDate(date.getDate() - dayOffset);
        sessionStorage.currentDate = date.getMonth() + 1 + '/' +
                                     date.getDate() + '/' +
                                     date.getFullYear();
        refreshEntries();
    });
    var shortName = 'Kilo';
    var version = '1.0';
    var displayName = 'Kilo';
    var maxSize = 65536;
    db = openDatabase(shortName, version, displayName, maxSize);
    db.transaction(
        function(transaction) {
            transaction.executeSql(
                'CREATE TABLE IF NOT EXISTS entries ' +
                '    (id INTEGER NOT NULL PRIMARY KEY AUTOINCREMENT, ' +
                '    date DATE NOT NULL, food TEXT NOT NULL, ' +
                '    calories INTEGER NOT NULL);'
            );
        }
    );
});
function saveSettings() {
    localStorage.age = $('#age').val();
    localStorage.budget = $('#budget').val();
    localStorage.weight = $('#weight').val();
    jQT.goBack();
    return false;
}
function loadSettings() {
    if (!localStorage.age) {
        localStorage.age = "";
    }
    if (!localStorage.budget) {
        localStorage.budget = "";
    }
    if (!localStorage.weight) {
        localStorage.weight = "";
    }
    $('#age').val(localStorage.age);
    $('#budget').val(localStorage.budget);
    $('#weight').val(localStorage.weight);
}
```

```
function refreshEntries() {
    var currentDate = sessionStorage.currentDate;
    $('#date h1').text(currentDate);
    $('#date ul li:gt(0)').remove();
    db.transaction(
        function(transaction) {
            transaction.executeSql(
                'SELECT * FROM entries WHERE date = ? ORDER BY food;',
                [currentDate],
                function (transaction, result) {
                    for (var i=0; i < result.rows.length; i++) {
                        var row = result.rows.item(i);
                        var newEntryRow = $('#entryTemplate').clone();
                        newEntryRow.removeAttr('id');
                        newEntryRow.removeAttr('style');
                        newEntryRow.data('entryId', row.id);
                        newEntryRow.appendTo('#date ul');
                        newEntryRow.find('.label').text(row.food);
                        newEntryRow.find('.calories').text(row.calories);
                        newEntryRow.find('.delete').click(function(){
                            var clickedEntry = $(this).parent();
                            var clickedEntryId = clickedEntry.data('entryId');
                            deleteEntryById(clickedEntryId);
                            clickedEntry.slideUp();
                        });
                    }
                },
                errorHandler
            );
        }
    );
}
function createEntry() {
    var date = sessionStorage.currentDate;
    var calories = $('#calories').val();
    var food = $('#food').val();
    db.transaction(
        function(transaction) {
            transaction.executeSql(
                'INSERT INTO entries (date, calories, food) VALUES (?, ?, ?);',
                [date, calories, food],
                function(){
                    refreshEntries();
                    jQT.goBack();
                },
                errorHandler
            );
        }
    );
    return false;
}
```

```
function errorHandler(transaction, error) {
    alert('Oops. Error was '+error.message+' (Code '+error.code+')');
    return true;
}
function deleteEntryById(id) {
    db.transaction(
        function(transaction) {
            transaction.executeSql('DELETE FROM entries WHERE id=?;',
                [id], null, errorHandler);
        }
    );
}
```

Web Database Error Code Reference

An error in the SQL database API will be reported with a callback containing one of the codes shown in Table 5-1.

Table 5-1. Web database error codes

Constant	Code	Situation
UNKNOWN_ERR	0	The transaction failed for reasons unrelated to the database itself and is not covered by any other error code.
DATABASE_ERR	1	The statement failed for database reasons not covered by any other error code.
VERSION_ERR	2	The operation failed because the actual database version was not what it should be. For example, a statement found that the actual database version no longer matches the expected version of the Database or DatabaseSync object, or the Database.changeVersion() or DatabaseSync.changeVersion() methods were passed a version that doesn't match the actual database version.
TOO_LARGE_ERR	3	The statement failed because the data returned from the database was too large. The SQL LIMIT modifier might be useful to reduce the size of the result set.
QUOTA_ERR	4	The statement failed because there was not enough remaining storage space, or the storage quota was reached and the user declined to give more space to the database.
SYNTAX_ERR	5	The statement failed because of a syntax error, the number of arguments did not match the number of ? placeholders in the statement, the statement tried to use a statement that is not allowed, such as BEGIN, COMMIT, or ROLLBACK, or the statement tried to use a verb that could modify the database when the transaction was read-only.
CONSTRAINT_ERR	6	An INSERT, UPDATE, or REPLACE statement failed due to a constraint failure. For example, because a row was being inserted and the value given for the primary key column duplicated the value of an existing row.
TIMEOUT_ERR	7	A lock for the transaction could not be obtained in a reasonable time.

What You've Learned

In this chapter, you learned two ways to store user data on the client: Web Storage and Web SQL Database. The Web SQL Database in particular opens up a world of possibilities for web-based application developers.

The only thing stopping us from running this example application in offline mode is that we have to initially connect to the web server each time the app is launched to download the HTML and related resources. Wouldn't it be schweet if we could just cache all that stuff locally on the device? Yeah, it would.

CHAPTER 6

Going Offline

There's a feature of HTML5 called the *offline application cache* that allows users to run web apps even when they are not connected to the Internet. It works like this: when a user navigates to your web app, the browser downloads and stores all the files it needs to display the page (HTML, CSS, JavaScript, images, etc.). The next time the user navigates to your web app, the browser will recognize the URL and serve the files out of the local application cache instead of pulling them across the network.

The Basics of the Offline Application Cache

The main component of the offline application cache is a *cache manifest file* that you host on your web server. I'm going to use a simple example to explain the concepts involved, then I'll show you how to apply what you've learned to the Kilo example we've been working on.

A manifest file is just a simple text document that lives on your web server and is sent to the user's device with a content type of `cache-manifest`. The manifest contains a list of files a user's device must download and save in order to function. Consider a web directory containing the following files:

```
index.html
logo.jpg
scripts/demo.js
styles/screen.css
```

In this case, *index.html* is the page users will load in their browsers when they visit the application. The other files are referenced from within *index.html*. To make everything available offline, you'd create a file named *demo.manifest* in the directory with *index.html* (don't bother creating this just yet; you'll see how to apply this to your app shortly). Here's a directory listing showing the added file:

```
demo.manifest
index.html
logo.jpg
scripts/demo.js
styles/screen.css
```

Next, you'd add the following lines to *demo.manifest*:

```
CACHE MANIFEST
index.html
logo.jpg
scripts/demo.js
styles/screen.css
```

> The paths in the manifest are relative to the location of the manifest file. You can also use absolute URLs like so:
>
> ```
> CACHE MANIFEST
> http://www.example.com/index.html
> http://www.example.com/logo.jpg
> http://www.example.com/scripts/demo.js
> http://www.example.com/styles/screen.css
> ```

Now that the manifest file is created, you'd need to link to it by adding a manifest attribute to the HTML tag inside *index.html*:

```
<html manifest="demo.manifest">
```

> We'll be using a PHP script to generate a *dynamic manifest file* for the Kilo app later in this chapter. The nice thing about PHP scripts is that they can specify their content type. So, unless you want to experiment with manifest files on your server, you can skip the following configuration step.

You must serve the manifest file with the `text/cache-manifest` content type or the browser will not recognize it:

Apache
If you are using the Apache web server, you can accomplish this by adding an *.htaccess* file to your web directory with the following line:

```
AddType text/cache-manifest .manifest
```

If you're on a Mac, see "Mac OS X and the .htaccess File" on page 106 for special instructions on enabling the use of the `AddType` directive in this file.

IIS (Windows)
If you are using the IIS browser on Windows, run the Internet Information Services (IIS) Manager, locate your web site under Connections (on the left), and click it. Next, double-click MIME Types, and use the Add action to associate the *manifest* file extension with it. If IIS tells you that a MIME type for that extension already

exists, you can either use a different file extension for your web app manifests (maybe `webmanifest` as shown in Figure 6-1) or double-click the existing entry for `manifest` and change it to the `text/cache-manifest` MIME type.

Web Hosting Provider

If your website is hosted by a web hosting provider, your provider may have a control panel for your website where you can add the appropriate MIME type.

Other

If the *.htaccess* file doesn't work for you, please refer to the portion of your web server documentation that pertains to *MIME types*. You must associate the file extension *.manifest* with the MIME type of `text/cache-manifest`.

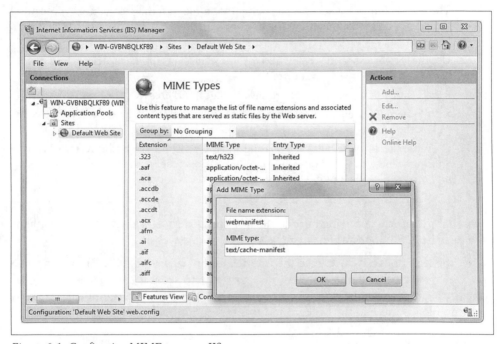

Figure 6-1. Configuring MIME types on IIS

Our offline application cache is now in working order. The next time a user browses to *http://example.com/index.html*, the page and its resources will load normally over the network (replace *example.com/index.html* with the URL of your web app). In the background, all the files listed in the manifest will be downloaded locally. Once the download completes and the user refreshes the page, he'll be accessing the local files only. He can now disconnect from the Internet and continue to access the web app.

Now that the user is accessing our files locally on his device, we have a new problem: how does he get updates when we make changes to the website?

When the user does have access to the Internet and navigates to the URL of your web app, his browser checks the manifest file on the site to see if it still matches the local copy. If the remote manifest has changed, the browser downloads all the files listed in it. It downloads these in the background to a temporary cache.

The comparison between the local manifest and the remote manifest is a byte-by-byte comparison of the file contents (including comments and blank lines). The file modification timestamp or changes to any of the resources themselves are irrelevant when determining whether or not changes have been made.

If something goes wrong during the download (e.g., the user loses his Internet connection), the partially downloaded temporary cache is automatically discarded and the previous one remains in effect. If the download is successful, the new local files will be used the next time the user launches the app.

Remember that when a manifest is updated, the download of the new files takes place in the background *after* the initial launch of the app. This means that even after the download completes, the user will still be working with the old files. In other words, the currently loaded page and all of its related files don't automatically reload when the download completes. The new files that were downloaded in the background will not become visible until the user relaunches the app.

This is very similar to standard desktop app update behavior. You launch an app, it tells you that updates are available, you click Download Updates, the download completes, and you are prompted to relaunch the app for the updates to take effect.

If you want to implement this sort of behavior in your app, you can listen for the `updateready` event of the `window.applicationCache` object, as described in "The JavaScript Console" on page 118, and notify the user however you like.

Online Whitelist and Fallback Options

It is possible to force the browser to always access certain resources over the network (this process is known as *whitelisting*). This means the browser will not cache them locally and they will not be available when the user is offline. To specify a resource as online only, use the `NETWORK:` keyword (the trailing : is essential) in the manifest file like so:

```
CACHE MANIFEST
index.html
scripts/demo.js
styles/screen.css

NETWORK:
logo.jpg
```

This whitelists *logo.jpg* by moving it into the `NETWORK` section of the manifest file. When the user is offline, the image will show up as a broken image link (Figure 6-2). When he is online, it will appear normally (Figure 6-3).

If you don't want offline users to see the broken image, use the `FALLBACK` keyword to specify a fallback resource like so:

```
CACHE MANIFEST
index.html
scripts/demo.js
styles/screen.css

FALLBACK:
logo.jpg offline.jpg
```

Now, when the user is offline, he'll see *offline.jpg* (Figure 6-4), and when he's online, he'll see *logo.jpg* (Figure 6-5).

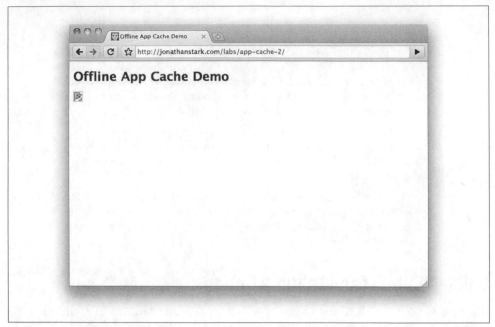

Figure 6-2. Whitelisted images will show up as broken links when the user is offline

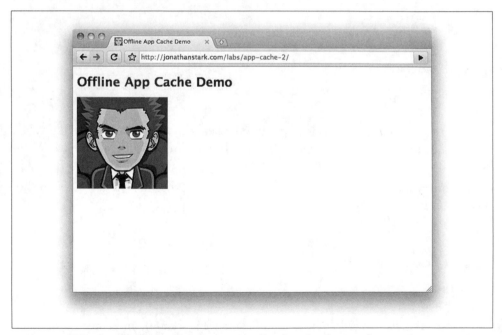

Figure 6-3. Whitelisted images will show up normally when the user is online

Figure 6-4. Fallback images will show up when the user is offline

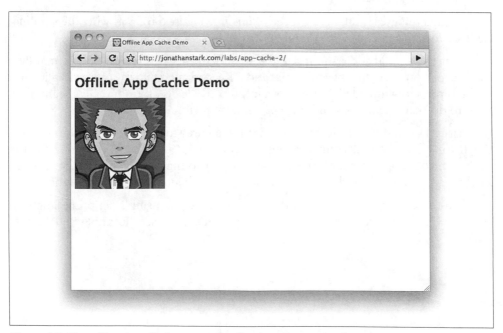

Figure 6-5. Hosted images will show up normally when the user is online

It's worth noting that you don't have to additionally list *offline.jpg* to the `CACHE MANIFEST` section. It will automatically be stored locally by virtue of being listed in the `FALLBACK` section of the manifest.

This becomes even more useful when you consider that you can specify a single fallback for multiple resources by using a *partial path*. Let's say I add an `images` directory to my website and put some files in it:

```
/demo.manifest
/index.html
/images/logo.jpg
/images/logo2.jpg
/images/offline.jpg
/scripts/demo.js
/styles/screen.css
```

I can now tell the browser to fall back to *offline.jpg* for anything contained in the `images` directory like so:

```
CACHE MANIFEST
index.html
scripts/demo.js
styles/screen.css

FALLBACK:
images/ images/offline.jpg
```

Now, when the user is offline, he'll see *offline.jpg* (Figure 6-6), and when he's online, he'll see *logo.jpg* and *logo2.jpg* (Figure 6-7).

Whether you should add resources to the `NETWORK` or `FALLBACK` sections of the manifest file depends on the nature of your application. Keep in mind that the offline application cache is primarily intended to store apps locally on a device. It's not really meant to be used to decrease server load, increase performance, etc.

In most cases you should be listing all of the files required to run your app in the manifest file. If you have a lot of dynamic content and you are not sure how to reference it in the manifest, your app is probably not a good fit for the offline application cache and you might want to consider a different approach (e.g., a client-side database, perhaps).

In the next section, you'll create a dynamic manifest file using a scripting language called PHP. If your web server doesn't have PHP installed, see "Running PHP Scripts on Your Web Server" on page 112.

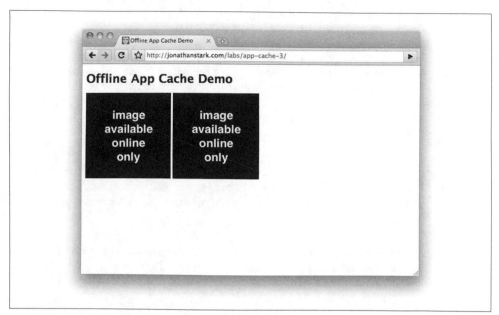

Figure 6-6. A single fallback image will show up in place of multiple images when the user is offline

Figure 6-7. Hosted images will show up normally when the user is online

Running PHP Scripts on Your Web Server

PHP is a versatile web-scripting language, and is supported by most web hosting providers. So, on most web servers, you can create a file whose name ends with the extension *.php*, add some PHP code to it, visit it in your web browser, and it will just work. If you've been using a web server on your personal computer to serve up pages to your Android phone, you'll need to get set up to run PHP scripts:

Windows

If you're running Microsoft's IIS web server, you must enable CGI services as described in "Running a Web Server Locally" on page 14. Next, go to *http://php.iis .net/* and click Install PHP to use the Microsoft Web Platform Installer to install PHP. If you're on Windows but not using IIS, see *http://php.net/manual/en/install .windows.php*.

Linux

PHP is easy to install on Linux. For example, Ubuntu users can type sudo apt-get install apache2 php5 at a shell prompt. To enable PHP in a user's personal *public_html* directory, edit the file */etc/apache2/mods-available/php5.conf* as root and follow the instructions inside it to enable PHP in user directories.

Mac OS X

Macs come with PHP installed, but you need to enable it:

1. Open Applications→ Utilities→Terminal and type these commands (you'll need to type your password when prompted):

   ```
   cd /etc/apache2
       sudo pico httpd.conf
   ```

2. Press Control-W. This brings up the option to search the file. Type php5 and press Return. This brings you to a line that should look like this:

   ```
   #LoadModule php5_module        libexec/apache2/libphp5.so
   ```

3. Using the arrow keys, move to the beginning of the line and delete the # comment character, which is preventing this line from having any effect.

4. Press Control-X to exit, answer Y to save changes, and press Return to save the file.

5. Next, start System Preferences, go to Sharing and, if needed, click the lock icon labeled "Click the lock to make changes" and type your password when prompted.

6. Clear the checkbox next to Web Sharing and then check it again. Now PHP should be enabled on your Mac's web server.

Now you're ready to test out PHP. Create a file in your web server's document directory (see "Running a Web Server Locally" on page 14) named *test.php* with these contents:

```
<?php
    phpinfo();
    ?>
```

Finally, visit one of the following URLs in your browser: if you're using the web server's document root, go to *http://localhost/test.php*; if you're using your user directory, go to *http://localhost/~YOURUSERNAME/test.php* (replace *YOURUSERNAME* with your username, but don't delete the ~; you can discover your username at the Terminal by typing echo $USER and pressing Return). If PHP is working, you'll see a table displaying your PHP version number and a lot of other information about your PHP installation. If it is not working, you'll see nothing but a blank page. Visit *http://www.php.net/support.php* for links to documentation and help with using PHP.

Creating a Dynamic Manifest File

Now that you're comfortable with how the offline app cache works, let's apply it to the Kilo example we've been working on. Kilo consists of quite a few files and manually listing them all in a manifest file would be a pain. Plus, a single typo would invalidate the entire manifest file and prevent the application from working offline.

To address this issue, we're going to write a little PHP file that reads the contents of the application directory (and subdirectories) and creates the file list for us. Create a new file in your Kilo directory named *manifest.php* and add the following code:

```php
<?php
  header('Content-Type: text/cache-manifest');❶
  echo "CACHE MANIFEST\n";❷

  $dir = new RecursiveDirectoryIterator(".");❸
  foreach(new RecursiveIteratorIterator($dir) as $file) {❹
    if ($file->IsFile() &&❺
        $file->getFilename() != "manifest.php" &&
        substr($file->getFilename(), 0, 1) != "." &&
        !strpos($file, DIRECTORY_SEPARATOR . '.'))❻
    {
      $file_name = $file->getPathName();
      if (DIRECTORY_SEPARATOR == "\\") {
        $file_name = strtr($file_name, '\\', '/');❼
      }
      echo $file_name . "\n";❽
    }
  }
?>
```

❶ The PHP header function outputs this file with the cache-manifest content type. Doing this is an alternative to using an *.htaccess* file to specify the content type for the manifest file. In fact, if you created an *.htaccess* file in "The Basics of the Offline Application Cache" on page 104, you can remove it if you are not using it for any other purpose.

❷ As I mentioned earlier in this chapter, the first line of a cache manifest file must be CACHE MANIFEST. As far as the browser is concerned, this is the first line of the document; the PHP file runs on the web server and the browser only sees the output of commands that emit text, such as echo.

❸ This line creates an object called $dir, which enumerates all the files in the current directory. It does so recursively, which means that if you have any files in subdirectories, it will find them, too.

❹ Each time the program passes through this loop, it sets the variable $file to an object that represents one of the files in the current directory. In English, this line would be, "Each time through, set the file variable to the next file found in the current directory or its subdirectories."

❺ The if statement here makes sure the file is actually a file (and not a directory or symbolic link) and ignores files named *manifest.php* or any file that starts with a . (such as *.htaccess*) or is contained in a directory that begins with a . (such as *.svn*).

 The leading ./ (.\ on Windows) is part of the file's full path; the . refers to the current directory and the / (\ on Windows) separates elements of the file's path. So there's always a ./ that appears before the filename in the output. However, when you check for a leading . in the filename, use the getFilename function, which returns the filename without the leading path. This way, you can detect files beginning with a . even if they are buried in a subdirectory.

❻ This part of the if statement needs a bit more explanation. It searches the file for any occurrence of /. (Linux or Mac) or \. (Windows). The PHP constant DIRECTORY_SEPARATOR is set to whatever (/ or \) directory separator is used on your operating system. Here's what is special about a directory separator followed by a dot: this indicates any filename in any subdirectory that begins with a dot, including something like *themes/.hidden/secret*.

❼ Although Windows is just fine using \ as a directory separator, web browsers use a / to separate directories. This uses the string translate function to replace the \ character with /. The reason that \ is doubled up here is that this character is also used as an escape character to impart special meaning (such as \n for a newline) to the character that follows. By doubling it up, you tell PHP to treat it as a real \.

❽ This section displays each file's name.

To the browser, *manifest.php* will look like this:

```
CACHE MANIFEST
./index.html
./jqtouch/jqtouch.css
./jqtouch/jqtouch.js
./jqtouch/jquery-1.4.2.js
./jqtouch/jquery.js
./kilo.css
```

```
./kilo.js
./themes/apple/img/activeButton.png
./themes/apple/img/backButton.png
./themes/apple/img/cancel.png
./themes/apple/img/chevron.png
./themes/apple/img/grayButton.png
./themes/apple/img/greenButton.png
./themes/apple/img/listArrowSel.png
./themes/apple/img/listGroup.png
./themes/apple/img/loading.gif
./themes/apple/img/on_off.png
./themes/apple/img/pinstripes.png
./themes/apple/img/redButton.png
./themes/apple/img/selection.png
./themes/apple/img/thumb.png
./themes/apple/img/toggle.png
./themes/apple/img/toggleOn.png
./themes/apple/img/toolbar.png
./themes/apple/img/toolButton.png
./themes/apple/img/whiteButton.png
./themes/apple/theme.css
./themes/default/img/backButton.png
./themes/default/img/backButtonActive.png
./themes/default/img/bigButton.png
./themes/default/img/bigButtonActive.png
./themes/default/img/button.png
./themes/default/img/buttonActive.png
./themes/default/img/chevron.png
./themes/default/img/chevronActive.png
./themes/default/img/chevronCircle.png
./themes/default/img/chevronCircleActive.png
./themes/default/img/loading.gif
./themes/default/img/toggleSwitch.png
./themes/default/img/toolbarBackground.png
./themes/default/theme.css
./themes/jqt/img/activeButton.png
./themes/jqt/img/back_button.png
./themes/jqt/img/back_button_clicked.png
./themes/jqt/img/blueButton.png
./themes/jqt/img/button.png
./themes/jqt/img/button_clicked.png
./themes/jqt/img/chevron.png
./themes/jqt/img/chevron_circle.png
./themes/jqt/img/grayButton.png
./themes/jqt/img/greenButton.png
./themes/jqt/img/loading.gif
./themes/jqt/img/on_off.png
./themes/jqt/img/redButton.png
./themes/jqt/img/rowhead.png
./themes/jqt/img/toggle.png
./themes/jqt/img/toggleOn.png
./themes/jqt/img/toolbar.png
./themes/jqt/img/whiteButton.png
./themes/jqt/theme.css
```

Try loading the page yourself in a browser (be sure to load it with an HTTP URL such as *http://localhost/~YOURUSERNAME/manifest.php*). If your browser tries to download it as a file, you can either try another browser (such as Chrome) or temporarily change `header('Content-Type: text/cache-manifest');` to `header('Content-Type: text/plain');` and then change it back when you're done looking at the results.

> If you see a lot more files in your listing, you may have some extraneous files from the jQTouch distribution. The files *LICENSE.txt*, *README.txt*, and *sample.htaccess* are safe to delete, as are the directories *demos* and *extensions*. If you see a number of directories named *.svn*, you may also safely delete them (unless you have put your working directory under the SVN version control system, in which case these files are important). Files beginning with a **.** will not be visible in the Mac OS X Finder or Linux File Manager (but you can work with them at the command line).

Now open *index.html* and add a reference to *manifest.php* in the head element like so:

```
<html manifest="manifest.php">
```

Now that the manifest is generated dynamically, let's modify it so its contents change when any of the files in the directory change (remember that the client will only re-download the application if the *manifest's contents* have changed). Here is the modified *manifest.php*:

```php
<?php
  header('Content-Type: text/cache-manifest');
  echo "CACHE MANIFEST\n";

  $hashes = "";①

  $dir = new RecursiveDirectoryIterator(".");
  foreach(new RecursiveIteratorIterator($dir) as $file) {
    if ($file->IsFile() &&
        $file->getFilename() != "manifest.php" &&
        substr($file->getFilename(), 0, 1) != "." &&
        !strpos($file, DIRECTORY_SEPARATOR . '.'))
    {
      $file_name = $file->getPathName();
      if (DIRECTORY_SEPARATOR == "\\") {
        $file_name = strtr($file_name, '\\', '/');
      }
      echo $file_name . "\n";
      $hashes .= md5_file($file);②
    }
  }
  echo "# Hash: " . md5($hashes) . "\n";③
?>
```

❶ This line initializes a string that will hold the *hashed* values of the files.

❷ This line computes the hash of each file using PHP's `md5_file` function (Message-Digest algorithm 5) and appends it to the end of the `$hashes` string. Any change to the file, however small, will also change the results of the `md5_file` function. The hash is a 32-character string, such as 4ac3c9c004cac7785fa6b132b4f18efc.

❸ This code takes the big string of hashes (all of the 32-character strings for each file concatenated together) and computes an MD5 hash of the string itself. This gives us a short (32-character instead of 32 multiplied by the number of files) string that's printed out as a comment (beginning with the comment symbol, #).

From the viewpoint of the client browser, there's nothing special about this line. It's a comment and the client browser ignores it. However, if one of the files is modified, this line will change, which means the manifest has changed.

Here's an example of what the manifest looks like with this change (some of the lines have been truncated for brevity):

```
CACHE MANIFEST
./index.html
./jqtouch/jqtouch.css
./jqtouch/jqtouch.js
...
./themes/jqt/img/toolbar.png
./themes/jqt/img/whiteButton.png
./themes/jqt/theme.css
# Hash: 0943176a145ca0a8067b58566e802499
```

The net result of all of this business is that changing a single character inside any file in the entire directory tree will insert a new hash string into the manifest. This means that any edits we make to any Kilo files will essentially modify the manifest file, which in turn will trigger a download the next time a user launches the app. Pretty nifty, eh?

Debugging

It can be tough to debug apps that use the offline application cache, because there's very little visibility into what is going on. You may find yourself constantly wondering if your files have downloaded or if you are viewing remote or local resources. Plus, switching your device between online and offline modes is not the snappiest procedure and can really slow down the develop-test-debug cycle.

One thing you can do to help determine what's going on when things aren't playing nice is to set up some console logging in JavaScript.

If you want to see what's happening from the web server's perspective, you can monitor its log files. For example, if you are running a web server on a Mac or Linux computer, you can open the command line and run these commands (the $ is the *shell prompt*, which you should not type):

```
$ cd /var/log/apache2/
$ tail -f access?log
```

This will display the web server's log entries, showing information such as the date and time a document was accessed, as well as the name of the document. When you are done, press Control-C to stop following the log.

The ? on the second line will match any character; on Ubuntu Linux, the filename is *access.log* and on the Mac it is *access_log*. If you are using another version of Linux, the name of the file and its location may be different.

On Windows, you can find IIS7's log files in *C:\inetpub\logs*, but you will need to authenticate as an administrative user to access the files (if you navigate to that folder in Windows Explorer, it will prompt you for administrative credentials).

The JavaScript Console

Adding the following JavaScript to your web apps during development will make your life a lot easier, and can actually help you internalize the process of what is going on. The following script will send feedback to the console (in Chrome, click the wrench icon and choose Tools→JavaScript Console) and free you from having to constantly refresh the browser window:

```javascript
// Convenience array of status values❶
var cacheStatusValues = [];
cacheStatusValues[0] = 'uncached';
cacheStatusValues[1] = 'idle';
cacheStatusValues[2] = 'checking';
cacheStatusValues[3] = 'downloading';
cacheStatusValues[4] = 'updateready';
cacheStatusValues[5] = 'obsolete';

// Listeners for all possible events❷
var cache = window.applicationCache;
cache.addEventListener('cached', logEvent, false);
cache.addEventListener('checking', logEvent, false);
cache.addEventListener('downloading', logEvent, false);
cache.addEventListener('error', logEvent, false);
cache.addEventListener('noupdate', logEvent, false);
cache.addEventListener('obsolete', logEvent, false);
cache.addEventListener('progress', logEvent, false);
cache.addEventListener('updateready', logEvent, false);
```

```
// Log every event to the console
function logEvent(e) { ❸
    var online, status, type, message;
    online = (navigator.onLine) ? 'yes' : 'no';
    status = cacheStatusValues[cache.status];
    type = e.type;
    message = 'online: ' + online;
    message+= ', event: ' + type;
    message+= ', status: ' + status;
    if (type == 'error' && navigator.onLine) {
        message+= ' (prolly a syntax error in manifest)';
    }
    console.log(message); ❹
}

// Swap in newly downloaded files when update is ready
window.applicationCache.addEventListener(
    'updateready',
    function(){
        window.applicationCache.swapCache();
        console.log('swap cache has been called');
    },
    false
);

// Check for manifest changes every 10 seconds
setInterval(function(){cache.update()}, 10000);
```

 You can store this in a *.js* file such as *debug.js* and refer to it in your HTML document via the `script` element's `src` attribute, as in `<script type="text/javascript" src="debug.js"></script>`.

This might look like a lot of code, but there really isn't that much going on here:

❶ The first seven lines set up an array of status values for the application cache object. There are six possible values defined by the HTML5 spec, and this code maps their integer values to a short description (i.e., status 3 means "downloading"). We include them to make the logging more descriptive down in the `logEvent` function.

❷ The next chunk of code sets up an event listener for every possible event defined by the spec. Each one calls the `logEvent` function.

❸ The `logEvent` function takes the event as input and makes a few simple calculations in order to compose a descriptive log message. If the event type is **error** and the user is online, there is probably a syntax error in the remote manifest. Syntax errors are extremely easy to make in the manifest, because all of the paths have to be valid. If you rename or move a file but forget to update the manifest, future updates will fail.

Using a dynamic manifest file helps avoid syntax errors. However, you have to watch that you don't include files (such as in a *.svn* sub-directory) that the server can't serve up due to permissions. This will make even a dynamic manifest fail, since the file ends up being unreadable.

❹ This line sends the composed message to the console.

If you load the web page in your browser and open the console, you'll see new messages appear every 10 seconds (Figure 6-8). If you don't see anything, change the contents of one of the files (or the name of a file) and reload the page in your browser *twice*. I strongly encourage you to play around with this until you have a feel for what's going on. You can tinker around with the manifest (e.g., change the contents and save it, rename it, move it to another directory) and watch the results of your actions pop into the console like magic.

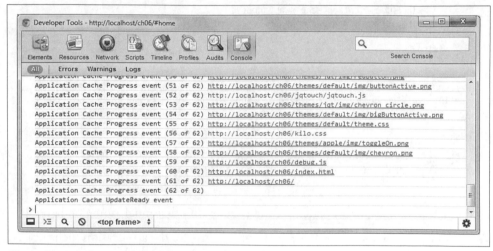

Figure 6-8. Use the console.log() function to send debugging messages to the JavaScript console

What You've Learned

In this chapter, you've learned how to give users access to a web app, even when they have no connection to the Internet. With this new addition to our programming tool-box, we now have the ability to create an offline app that is virtually indistinguishable from a native application downloaded from the Android Market.

Of course, a pure web app such as this is still limited by the security constraints that exist for all web apps. For example, a web app can't access the Address Book, the camera, vibration, or the accelerometer on the phone. In the next chapter, I'll address these issues and more with the assistance of an open source project called PhoneGap.

CHAPTER 7

Going Native

Our web app can now do many things that a native app can do: launch from the home screen, store data locally on the phone, and operate in offline mode. We've formatted it nicely for the device and set up native-looking animations to provide feedback and context to the user.

However, there are still two things that it cannot do: it can't access the device features and hardware (e.g., geolocation, accelerometer, sound, and vibration) and it can't be submitted to the Android Market. In this chapter, you will learn how to extend the reach of your web app beyond the normal confines of the browser using an open source project called PhoneGap.

Introduction to PhoneGap

The mobile landscape is littered with devices, platforms, and operating systems. If you are a web developer, you might be familiar with the agony of testing 10 or so browser versions across 10 or so operating system versions. Multiply that by 100 and you have mobile. There is simply no cost-effective way to develop and test across all of the possible combinations.

Enter PhoneGap. PhoneGap is an open source development tool created by Nitobi (*http://www.nitobi.com/*; now part of Adobe) that acts as a unified bridge between web apps and mobile device APIs. It consists of a native app project template for each of the major platforms, where each project is just a bare-bones web browser with heightened permissions. What this means in concrete terms is that PhoneGap makes it possible to access the accelerometer, camera, microphone, speakers, and more using simple JavaScript calls.

Furthermore, the resulting app—although written by you with HTML, CSS, and Java-Script—is encased in a native app and you can submit it to the respective app store for the platforms in question. Currently, iPhone, Android, Windows Phone, BlackBerry, webOS, bada, and Symbian are supported, and Qt is in development.

Of course, different devices have different features. Maybe a particular device doesn't have a camera or doesn't have an accelerometer. Even when devices do have the same features, they each have their own ways of exposing these features to the developer. PhoneGap abstracts the APIs for the most widely available mobile phone features so mobile application developers can use the same code everywhere.

There are other tools available that are often compared to PhoneGap, such as RhoMobile (*http://rhomobile.com/*) and Titanium Mobile (*http://www.appcelerator.com/*). While these tools all promote cross-platform mobile development and are marketed at web designers and developers, there are fundamental difference between them. PhoneGap is the only tool that allows you to write a standard web app and drop it into a native code environment virtually unchanged.

Every other product that I've looked at requires you to write code based on a proprietary framework that outputs native code (i.e., you aren't writing HTML, CSS, and JavaScript that would run in a browser). It's beyond the scope of this book to do an in-depth comparison, but I did write a post (*www.netmagazine.com/features/developers-guide-mobile -frameworks*) on this topic. You might want to check it out in case another tool suits your needs better than PhoneGap.

Since this is an Android book, we'll focus on the Android branch of PhoneGap. Just be aware that you could potentially deploy your app to iOS, Windows Phone, BlackBerry, and other popular devices with little or no modification.

There are two ways to use PhoneGap. You can either set up a local development environment or use the PhoneGap Build service to compile in the cloud. Developing locally gives you more control and is completely free, but requires some initial setup. Compiling with PhoneGap Build is zero install and very easy to use, but prolongs the code/compile/install/test cycle. And although Build is very inexpensive, it's not free. In this chapter, I'll cover how to build your apps with a local development environment. For more information about PhoneGap Build, see *https://build.phonegap.com*.

Building Your App Locally with Eclipse and the Android SDK

Download and Install Eclipse Classic

Eclipse is an open source integrated development environment (IDE). It's used by software developers to write, compile, and debug all sorts of projects. There is nothing about it that is specific to Android; once we get Eclipse installed, we'll configure it to use Android SDK tools. But first things first...here's how you get Eclipse:

1. Navigate to *http://www.eclipse.org/downloads/* in your web browser.
2. Select your platform (Mac, Windows, or Linux) from the popup list.

3. Locate **Eclipse Classic** in the list of packages and the download version appropriate for your machine (32 bit or 64 bit).

4. When the download completes, extract the archive to a convenient location on your hard drive. I've placed mine in the */Applications* directory on my Mac, but you can put it anywhere you like.

5. Navigate into the *eclipse* directory.

6. Double-click the Eclipse icon to launch Eclipse.

7. You'll be prompted to specify a workspace directory where Eclipse will store your projects. I've specified the */Users/jstark/Documents/workspace* directory on my Mac, but you can pick any directory you like. This setting can be modified later in Eclipse preferences under General→Startup and Shutdown→Workspaces.

We'll be modifying our Eclipse configuration in a bit but we have to download a few more things before continuing.

Download and Install the Android SDK

Now the we have Eclipse installed, we need the Android SDK.

1. Download the Android SDK appropriate for your system (Mac, Windows, Linux) from *http://developer.android.com/sdk/index.html*.

2. When the download completes, extract the archive to a convenient location on your hard drive. I've placed mine in the */Users/jstark* directory on my Mac, but you can put it anywhere you like. If you're running Windows, you can use the executable installer, which will install everything for you (when you reach the installer's final page, deselect Start SDK Manager before clicking Finish).

3. By default, the Android SDK directory is named in a platform specific fashion (e.g., *android-sdk-macosx*). For simplicity, I've renamed mine *android-sdk*.

Install the ADT Plug-In in Eclipse

Now we need to customize Eclipse for Android development. To do this, we need the Android Developer Tools (ADT) plug-in for Eclipse. Installation is done from within Eclipse itself:

1. Launch Eclipse if it's not already running.

2. Select Install New Software from the Help menu.

3. In the Install window that appears, click the Add button near the top right corner.

4. In the Add Repository window that appears, enter "ADT Plugin" in the name field and *https://dl-ssl.google.com/android/eclipse/* in the location field.

5. Click OK. After a few seconds, a Developer Tools entry should appear in the central area of the Install window. If it doesn't appear, try changing `https` to `http` in the location field.

6. Select the checkbox next to Developer Tools and click Next.

7. A list of tools to be downloaded should appear. Click Next.

8. Read and accept the license agreements, then click the Finish button.

9. When your download completes, restart Eclipse.

You must then configure the ADT plug-in like so:

1. Launch Eclipse if it's not already running.

2. Open the Eclipse Preferences dialog window by choosing Window→Preferences (on Mac, choose Eclipse→Preferences).

3. Select Android from the panel on the left.

4. Browse the location of your Android SDK. In my case, the resulting path is */Users/jstark/android-sdk/*. If you used the Windows installer, the default is *C:\Program Files\Android\android-sdk*.

5. Click the Apply button.

6. Click the OK button.

Add Android Platforms and Other Components

We're nearly done getting the development environment set up. Our next task is to download the tools, platforms, and extras for the Android platforms we want to target:

1. Launch Eclipse if it's not already running.

2. Select Android SDK Manager from the Window menu.

3. In the Android SDK window that appears, select Android SDK Platform-tools, Android 2.1 (you can choose an older version, but 2.1 is likely to guarantee compatibility with a large number of devices), and if available, the Google USB Driver Package under Extras.

4. Click the Install X Packages button. You should be presented with the Choose Packages to Install window.

5. After reading the license agreements click the "Accept All" radio button, then click the Install button.

6. If you are prompted to restart ADB, click Yes.

7. If you are alerted that updates are available, follow the instructions given.

You may see "Access is denied" error messages on Windows. If this happens, locate the *C:\Program Files\Android* folder in Windows Explorer, and right-click on the folder, choose Properties→Security, and then click Edit→Add, type your username, click OK, then allow Full Control and click OK. Try installing the packages again.

Download the Latest Copy of PhoneGap

We now have a stock Android development environment set up. Our next task is to download the PhoneGap project files:

1. Download the latest copy of PhoneGap from *http://www.phonegap.com/download*.

2. When the download completes, extract the archive to a convenient location on your hard drive. I've placed mine in the */Users/jstark/Desktop* directory on my Mac, but you can put it anywhere you like.

3. By default, the PhoneGap directory includes a version number in the name (e.g., *callback-phonegap-c81c02b*). For convenience and clarity, I've renamed mine *PhoneGap*.

4. Open the PhoneGap directory. There is a bunch of cool stuff in there but we only need to worry about the Android directory. It contains the Android branch of the PhoneGap project and has a couple of files we'll need to add to our project in Eclipse.

Note that PhoneGap for Android is not an Eclipse plug-in or anything fancy like that. It's basically an empty Android project template from which we'll cherry-pick some code for use in our project.

Set Up a New Android Project

We're finally ready to create our first project!

1. Launch Eclipse, then select New→Android Project from the File Menu. If Android Project is not an option, select New→Project from the File menu to call up the New Project window and select Android Project from the Android folder.

2. Specify a name for the project in the Project Name field. This is the name that will be used to save your project locally in your workspace and is not the app name that your users will see. I've entered KiloForAndroid as my project name.

3. Make sure the "Create new project in workspace" radio button is checked. You can leave the other settings alone and click the Next button.

4. You will be presented with the Select build target window. Make sure Android 2.1 is checked and click the Next button. (You can choose an older or newer SDK, but 2.1 is likely to guarantee compatibility with a large number of devices.)

5. You will be presented with the Application Info window. Specify a name for your app (this is the name your users will see). I've entered Kilo.

6. Specify a package name for your app using reverse domain name syntax. I've entered `com.jonathanstark.kilo` but you should use your own reverse domain name (i.e., don't use *jonathanstark* in yours).

7. Make sure Create Activity is checked and type **App** in the field provided. This is the name that will be given to the initial class for your application.

8. You can leave the rest of the settings in this window alone and click the Finish button.

Once the create process completes, you should see the `KiloForAndroid` project appear in Package Explorer panel in Eclipse. At this point, it's just a standard Android project. Now we need to add PhoneGap to the mix by grabbing some code from the PhoneGap files we downloaded and adding it to our project:

1. In the root level of the project, create a new folder called */libs*. You can do this by right clicking on the *KiloForAndroid* folder in the Package Explorer panel and selecting New→Folder in the contextual menu that appears.

2. In the */assets* folder of the project, create a new folder called *www*.

3. Copy *phonegap-x.x.x.jar* from your *PhoneGap/Android* directory to */libs* (you can just drag the file into the */libs* directory in Package Explorer).

4. Find *phonegap-x.x.x.js* in your *PhoneGap/Android* directory, rename it to *phonegap.js*, and copy it to */assets/www*.

5. Copy *xml* from your *PhoneGap/Android* directory to */res*.

6. Right click on the */libs* folder and go to Build Path→Configure Build Path.

7. You will be presented with the Properties window. Click on the Libraries tab.

8. Click on the Add JARs button.

9. In the JAR Selection window that appears, select */KiloForAndroid/libs/phonegap-x.x.x.jar* and click the OK button, then click OK again to close the Properties window.

10. Locate */src/YOUR_PACKAGE_NAME/App.java* in the Package Explorer and double click it to open in the central Code Editor panel.

11. Add the following line after `import android.os.Bundle;`:

    `import com.phonegap.*;`

12. Change the class's extend from `Activity` to `DroidGap`.

13. Delete the following line:

    `import android.app.Activity;`

14. Replace the `setContentView(R.layout.main);` line with the following:

    `super.loadUrl("file:///android_asset/www/index.html");`

15. Select Save from the File menu to save your changes.

Running Kilo as an Android App

Now you're almost ready to try running Kilo as an app. First, drag all the files that make up your Kilo app (*index.html*, *kilo.css*, *kilo.js*, as well as the *jqtouch* and *themes* folders) to the *assets/www* directory in Eclipse's package manager. Once you've done this, you can edit any of those files in Eclipse by double-clicking them, or if needed, right-clicking them and choosing Open With→Text Editor. Note that from here on out, you'll be working with the copies of these files that are stored in the Eclipse project, not the originals from earlier chapters. Next, you'll need to make a few changes to some files:

index.html

Open *index.html* for editing: locate it in Eclipse's Package Explorer under `assets/www`. Right-click *index.html*, then choose Open With→Text Editor so you don't open it in a web browser (the next time you need to open it, you can just double-click it, since Eclipse will remember your preference):

1. Remove the reference to *manifest.php* from the `head` element in *index.html* (change it from `<html manifest="manifest.php">` to `<html>`).

2. Add a line to pull in *phonegap.js* just before you pull in *kilo.js*:

   ```
   <script type="text/javascript" src="phonegap.js"></script>
   <script type="text/javascript" src="kilo.js"></script>
   ```

3. If you enabled *debug.js* in "The JavaScript Console" on page 118, edit *index.html* and remove the `script` tag that loads it.

AndroidManifest.xml

On Android, PhoneGap uses a WebView object to host your application. By default, the WebView resets its state when you rotate the device. You can add an option to the AndroidManifest to handle rotation gracefully. Locate *Android-Manifest.xml* in the Package Explorer and double-click it. Next, click the AndroidManifest.xml tab at the bottom of the Android Manifest page to edit its raw XML. Finally, add the `android:configChanges="keyboardHidden|orientation"` attribute to the `activity` tag like so:

   ```
   <activity
       android:configChanges="keyboardHidden|orientation"
       android:label="@string/app_name"
       android:name=".App">
   ```

Before you try to run the app, make sure your Android device is set up for debugging (go into Settings, choose Applications→Development, and enable USB Debugging).

Next, plug your Android device into your computer with a USB connection. If you're on Windows, you'll probably need to configure the USB driver. See *http://developer.android.com/sdk/win-usb.html* for details and downloads. Then, choose Run→Run in Eclipse. Kilo should appear on your screen, but as a standalone app rather than in a web page (see Figure 7-1).

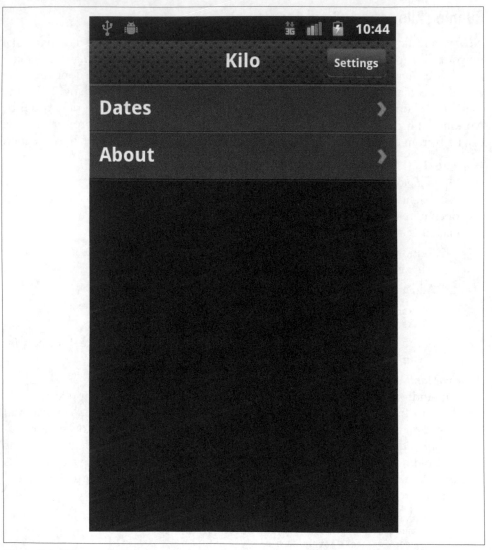

Figure 7-1. Kilo running as an app

If you have any trouble getting PhoneGap to run properly, check out the resources available at the PhoneGap project. The Community Page (*http://phonegap.com/community*) links to the wiki, Google Group, IRC channel, and more where you can find help from the community. PhoneGap also has support packages available (*http://phonegap.com/ support*).

Controlling the Phone with JavaScript

The stage is now set for us to start enhancing our application with calls to the native device features. Thanks to *phonegap.js*, all you have to do to make the phone vibrate for 200 milliseconds, for example, is to add a bit of JavaScript to your code:

```
navigator.notification.vibrate(200);
```

Pretty simple, right?

Beep, Vibrate, and Alert

PhoneGap makes beep, vibrate, and alert functions so simple that I'm going to lump them together into one example. Specifically, we'll set up the app to beep, vibrate, and display a custom alert when the user creates an entry that puts him over his daily calorie budget. To do so, add the following function to the end of the *kilo.js* (remember to edit the copy in Eclipse, not the original copy from the previous chapters):

```
function checkBudget() {❶
    var currentDate = sessionStorage.currentDate;
    var dailyBudget = localStorage.budget;
    db.transaction(❷
        function(transaction) {
            transaction.executeSql(❸
                'SELECT SUM(calories) AS currentTotal FROM entries WHERE date = ?;',❹
                [currentDate], ❺
                function (transaction, result) {❻
                    var currentTotal = result.rows.item(0).currentTotal;❼
                    if (currentTotal > dailyBudget) {❽
                        var overage = currentTotal - dailyBudget;❾
                        var message = 'You are '+overage+' calories over your '
                            + 'daily budget. Better start jogging!';❿
                        try {⓫
                            navigator.notification.beep(1);
                            navigator.notification.vibrate(200);
                        } catch(e){
                            // No equivalent in web app
                        }
                        try {⓬
                            navigator.notification.alert(message,
                                    null, 'Over Budget', 'Dang!');
                        } catch(e) {
                            alert(message);
                        }
                    }
                }
            },
            errorHandler⓭
        );
    }
    );
}
```

Here's the blow-by-blow description:

❶ This is the beginning of the `checkBudget()` function. It initializes the `currentDate` variable to the value stored in `sessionStorage` (i.e., the value entered by the user in the Settings panel) and sets the `dailyBudget` variable to the value stored in `localStorage` (i.e., the date the user taps on the Dates panel).

❷ Start a database transaction in preparation for calculating the total calories for the current date.

❸ Run the `executeSql()` method of the transaction object.

Let's examine the four parameters of the `executeSql()` method:

❹ The first parameter is a prepared SQL statement that uses the SUM function to add up all the values in the calories column for the entries that match the current date.

❺ The second parameter is a single-value array that will replace the question mark in the prepared statement on the previous line.

❻ The third parameter is an anonymous function that will be called if the SQL query completes successfully (we'll look at this in detail momentarily).

Here's what's going on in the anonymous function that was passed in as the third parameter:

❼ This line grabs the current total from the first row of the result. Since we are just asking for the sum of a column, the database is only going to return one row (i.e., this query will always return one row). Remember that the records of the result set are accessed with the `item()` method of the rows property of the result object, and that the rows are zero-based (meaning that the first row is 0).

❽ Check to see if the current calorie total for the day is greater than the daily budget specified on the Settings panel. If so, the block that follows will be executed.

❾ Calculate how far the user is over his calorie budget.

❿ Compose a message to display to the user.

⓫ This is a try/catch block that attempts to call the `beep()` and `vibrate()` methods of the navigator notification object. These methods only exist in PhoneGap, so if the user is running the app in a browser, these methods will fail and execution will jump to the catch block. Since there is no browser-based equivalent to beep or vibrate, the catch block has been left empty.

⓬ This is a try/catch block that attempts to call the `alert()` method of the navigator notification object. This method only exists in PhoneGap, so if the user is running the app in a browser, it will fail and execution will jump to the catch block. The browser-based equivalent to alert is a standard JavaScript alert, which is called as a fallback.

There are a couple of differences between the PhoneGap alert and the native JavaScript alert. For example, the PhoneGap alert allows you to specify a callback method (null, since we don't need it here), as well as the title and the button name (Figure 7-2); the JavaScript alert does not (Figure 7-3).

There is also a more subtle difference between the two alerts: the native JavaScript alert is modal and the PhoneGap alert is not. In other words, script execution will pause at the point when you call a native alert, whereas execution will continue with the PhoneGap version. This may or may not be a big deal depending on the nature of your application, so keep this distinction in mind.

⓭ The fourth parameter is the name of the generic SQL error handler that will be called in the event of a SQL error.

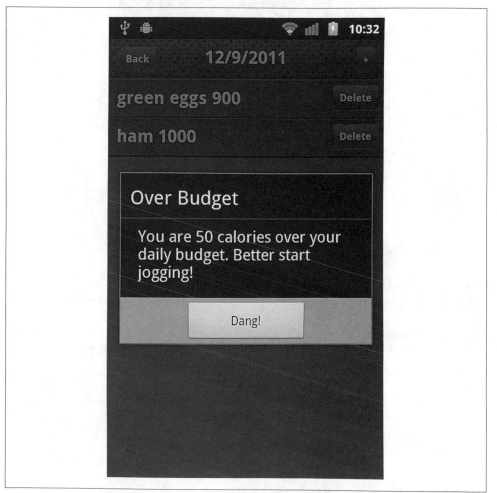

Figure 7-2. The PhoneGap alert allows you to specify the title and button label

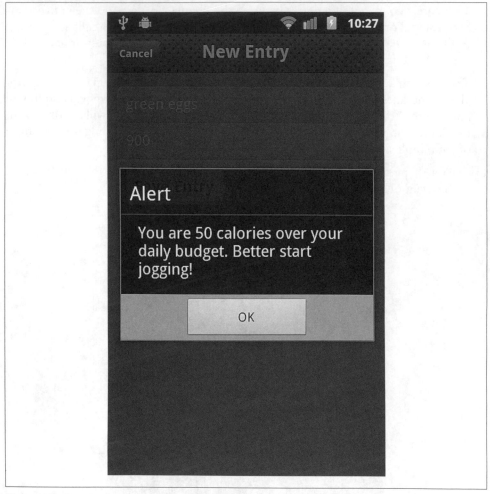

Figure 7-3. A native JavaScript alert does not allow you to specify the title and button label

With our `checkBudget()` function complete, we can now call it by adding a single line to the success callback of our `createEntry()` function:

```
function createEntry() {
    var date = sessionStorage.currentDate;
    var calories = $('#calories').val();
    var food = $('#food').val();
    db.transaction(
        function(transaction) {
            transaction.executeSql(
                'INSERT INTO entries (date, calories, food) VALUES (?, ?, ?);',
                [date, calories, food],
                function(){
                    refreshEntries();
```

```
                checkBudget();
                jQT.goBack();
            },
            errorHandler
        );
    }
    );
    return false;
}
```

After you've made these changes, save the *kilo.js* file, and then locate *Android Manifest.xml* in the Package Explorer and double-click it. Next, click the Android-Manifest.xml tab at the bottom of the Android Manifest page to edit its raw XML. Then, add the line shown in bold just below the `uses-sdk`:

```
<uses-sdk android:minSdkVersion="7" />
<uses-permission android:name="android.permission.VIBRATE"/>
```

That line gives your app permission to use the vibration function of the phone. Next, choose Run→Run in Eclipse to run the app. Try adding an entry that causes you to exceed your calorie budget to see what happens.

Geolocation

Let's update Kilo to save the location when entries are created. Once we have that information, we'll add a Map Location button that will open the built-in Maps application and drop a pin at the point where the entry was created.

The first step is to add latitude and longitude columns to the table to store the information. This is a great opportunity to show you how to upgrade your database on the fly. Remember the version number (1.0) we specified for the database in the `document ready` function? Now we can use that number to check whether the database is out of date, and if so, we'll upgrade it with a couple of `ALTER TABLE` statements. Each one of these statements adds a new column to the table: first `longitude`, then `latitude`. Make the following changes (shown in bold) to the part of the `document ready` function in *kilo.js* that opens the database:

```
var shortName = 'Kilo';
var version = '1.1';❶
var displayName = 'Kilo';
var maxSize = 65536;
db = openDatabase(shortName, '', displayName, maxSize);❷
if (db.version == '1.0') {❸
    db.changeVersion('1.0', version,❹
        function(transaction) {❺
            transaction.executeSql(❻
                'ALTER TABLE entries ' +
                '  ADD COLUMN longitude TEXT');
            transaction.executeSql(
                'ALTER TABLE entries ' +
                '  ADD COLUMN latitude TEXT');
        },
```

```
            function(e) {
                alert('DB upgrade error: ' + e.message);❼
            }
        );
    } else if (db.version == '') {❽
      db.changeVersion('', version);
    }

    db.transaction(
        function(transaction) {
            transaction.executeSql(
                'CREATE TABLE IF NOT EXISTS entries ' +
                '  (id INTEGER NOT NULL PRIMARY KEY AUTOINCREMENT, ' +
                '   date DATE NOT NULL, food TEXT NOT NULL, ' +
                '   calories INTEGER NOT NULL, ' +
                '   longitude TEXT, latitude TEXT);'❾
            );
        }
    );
```

❶ This line increments the database version to 1.1 since you're about to add a couple of columns to the entries table.

❷ Instead of specifying a revision when you open the database, leave the revision parameter blank. That will open any version of the database.

❸ This line checks to see if it's version 1.0 of the database.

❹ If it's version 1.0, you'll call the changeVersion function with four arguments. The first one is the version you're upgrading from, and the second is the new version number. Next comes a function that executes two ALTER TABLE statements: one to add the longitude column, the other to add the latitude column.

❺ Pass a callback function into the transaction, with the transaction object as its sole parameter.

❻ Call the executeSql() method of the transaction object.

❼ The last argument to changeVersion is a function to handle any errors (it pops up an alert message).

❽ If the database didn't exist already, then there's no old version of the database to upgrade. But because you opened the database without specifying a version, the version will be blank. The next line changes that blank version number to version "1.1".

❾ The CREATE TABLE won't run if the entries table already exists. But if it doesn't exist, you still need to create it. And you still need the latitude and longitude columns when you create the table, and this updated CREATE TABLE statement takes care of that.

Next, we'll rewrite the `createEntry()` function that we first saw in Chapter 5 to use the geolocation feature of the phone to determine the current latitude and longitude. Replace the existing `createEntry()` function in *kilo.js* with this:

```
function createEntry() {❶
    navigator.geolocation.getCurrentPosition(❷
        function(position){❸
            var latitude = position.coords.latitude;❹
            var longitude = position.coords.longitude;
            insertEntry(latitude, longitude);❺
        },
        function(){❻
            insertEntry();❼
        }
    );
    return false;❽
}
```

❶ Begin the `createEntry()` function.

❷ Call the `getCurrentPosition()` function of the `geolocation` object and pass it two callback functions: one for success and one for errors.

❸ This is the beginning of the success callback. Notice that it accepts a single parameter (i.e., `position`).

❹ These two lines grab the `latitude` and `longitude` coordinates out of the `position` object.

❺ Pass the `latitude` and `longitude` coordinates into a function called `insertEntry()`, which we'll look at momentarily.

❻ This is the beginning of the error callback.

❼ Because we're in the error callback, this will only be called if geolocation fails (for example, if the application can't determine the location), so call the `insertEntry()` function without parameters.

❽ Return `false` to prevent the default navigation behavior of clicking the form's Submit button.

Wondering where the SQL `INSERT` statement got to? Let's take a look at the `insertEntry()` function. This new function creates the entry in the database. Add the following to *kilo.js*:

```
function insertEntry(latitude, longitude) {❶
    var date = sessionStorage.currentDate;❷
    var calories = $('#calories').val();❸
    var food = $('#food').val();❹
    db.transaction(❺
        function(transaction) {❻
            transaction.executeSql(❼
                'INSERT INTO entries (date, calories, food, latitude, longitude) ' +
                    'VALUES (?, ?, ?, ?, ?);',❽
```

```
                    [date, calories, food, latitude, longitude],❾
                    function(){❿
                        refreshEntries();
                        checkBudget();
                        jQT.goBack();
                    },
                    errorHandler⓫
                );
            }
        );
    }
```

❶ The beginning of the insertEntry() function, allowing for latitude and longitude values to be passed in. Although there is no way to explicitly mark a parameter as optional in JavaScript, they will simply be undefined if they are not passed in.

❷ Get the currentDate out of sessionStorage. Remember that its value will be set when the user taps an item on the Dates panel to navigate to the Date panel. When he taps the + button to reveal the New Entry panel, this value will still be set to the currently selected Date panel item.

❸ Get the calories value out of the createEntry form.

❹ Get the food value out of the createEntry form.

❺ Begin a database transaction.

❻ Pass a callback function into the transaction, with the transaction object as its sole parameter.

❼ Call the executeSql() method of the transaction object.

❽ Define the SQL prepared statement with question marks as data placeholders.

❾ Pass an array of values for the placeholders. If latitude and longitude are not passed into the insertEntry() function, they will be undefined.

❿ Define the success callback function.

⓫ Define the error callback function.

To confirm that Kilo is actually saving these location values, we'll want to display them somewhere in the interface. Let's add an Inspect Entry panel to display the stored values. We'll include a Map Location button on the panel that will display where the entry was created. Add the following to *index.html*, right before the closing body tag (</body>):

```
    <div id="inspectEntry">
        <div class="toolbar">
            <h1>Inspect Entry</h1>
            <a class="button cancel" href="#">Cancel</a>
        </div>
        <form method="post">
            <ul class="rounded">
                <li><input type="text" placeholder="Food" name="food" value="" /></li>
```

```
        <li><input type="tel" placeholder="Calories"
            name="calories" value="" /></li>❶
        <li><input type="submit" value="Save Changes" /></li>
    </ul>
    <ul class="rounded">
        <li><input type="text" name="latitude" value="" /></li>❷
        <li><input type="text" name="longitude" value="" /></li>
        <li><p class="whiteButton" id="mapLocation">Map Location</p></li>❸
    </ul>
    </form>
</div>
```

This should look very similar to the New Entry panel that we first saw in "Adding the New Entry Panel" on page 68, so I'll just call out a couple of things:

❶ The input type has been set to `tel` to call the telephone keyboard when cursor is placed in the field. This is a bit of a hack, but I think it's worth it, because that keyboard is much more appropriate for a numeric data field.

❷ The latitude and longitude fields are editable and contained within the form, which means the user would be able to edit them. This probably would not make sense in the final application, but it makes it a lot easier to test during development because you can enter location values manually to test the Map Location button.

❸ This Map Location button won't do anything when clicked at this point; we'll add a click handler to it momentarily.

Now we need to give the user a way to navigate to this Inspect Entry panel, so we'll modify the behavior of the Date panel such that when the user taps an entry in the list, the Inspect Entry panel will slide up from the bottom of the screen.

The first step is to wire up the click event handler (which we'll create next), and also modify the way clicks on the Delete button are processed. Add the three highlighted changes below to the `refreshEntries()` function in *kilo.js*:

```
function refreshEntries() {
    var currentDate = sessionStorage.currentDate;
    $('#date h1').text(currentDate);
    $('#date ul li:gt(0)').remove();
    db.transaction(
        function(transaction) {
            transaction.executeSql(
                'SELECT * FROM entries WHERE date = ? ORDER BY food;',
                [currentDate],
                function (transaction, result) {
                    for (var i=0; i < result.rows.length; i++) {
                        var row = result.rows.item(i);
                        var newEntryRow = $('#entryTemplate').clone();
                        newEntryRow.removeAttr('id');
                        newEntryRow.removeAttr('style');
                        newEntryRow.data('entryId', row.id);
                        newEntryRow.appendTo('#date ul');
                        newEntryRow.find('.label').text(row.food);
                        newEntryRow.find('.calories').text(row.calories);
```

```
                    newEntryRow.find('.delete').click(function(e){❶
                        var clickedEntry = $(this).parent();
                        var clickedEntryId = clickedEntry.data('entryId');
                        deleteEntryById(clickedEntryId);
                        clickedEntry.slideUp();
                        e.stopPropagation();❷
                    });
                    newEntryRow.click(entryClickHandler);❸
                }
            },
            errorHandler
        );
    }
    );
}
```

❶ We have to add the e parameter (the event) to the function call in order to have access to the stopPropagation() method of the event, used shortly. If we didn't add the e parameter, e.stopPropagation() would be undefined.

❷ The e.stopPropagation(); added to the Delete button click handler tells the browser not to let the click event bubble up the DOM to parent elements. This is important because we've now added a click handler to the row itself (and the entry row is the parent of the Delete button). If we didn't call stopPropagation(), both the Delete button handler and the entryClickHandler would fire when the user tapped the Delete button.

❸ The newEntryRow.click(entryClickHandler); tells the browser to call the entryClick Handler function when the entry is tapped.

Now let's add the entryClickHandler() function to *kilo.js*:

```
function entryClickHandler(e){
    sessionStorage.entryId = $(this).data('entryId');❶
    db.transaction(❷
        function(transaction) {❸
            transaction.executeSql(❹
                'SELECT * FROM entries WHERE id = ?;', ❺
                [sessionStorage.entryId], ❻
                function (transaction, result) {❼
                    var row = result.rows.item(0);❽
                    var food = row.food;❾
                    var calories = row.calories;
                    var latitude = row.latitude;
                    var longitude = row.longitude;
                    $('#inspectEntry input[name="food"]').val(food);❿
                    $('#inspectEntry input[name="calories"]').val(calories);
                    $('#inspectEntry input[name="latitude"]').val(latitude);
                    $('#inspectEntry input[name="longitude"]').val(longitude);
                    $('#mapLocation').click(function(){⓫
                        window.location = 'http://maps.google.com/maps?z=15&q='+
                            food+'@'+latitude+','+longitude;
                    });
                    jQT.goTo('#inspectEntry', 'slideup');⓬
```

```
        },
        errorHandler🄭
    );
    }
  );
}
```

❶ Get the `entryId` from the entry that the user tapped and store it in session storage.

❷ Begin a database transaction.

❸ Pass a callback function into the transaction, with the transaction object as its sole parameter.

❹ Call the `executeSql()` method of the transaction object.

❺ Define the SQL prepared statement with a question mark as data placeholder.

❻ Pass a single element array for the placeholder.

❼ Begin the success callback function.

❽ Get the first (and only, since we're just querying for one entry) row of the result.

❾ Set some variables based on the values from the row.

❿ Set values of the form fields based on the variables.

⓫ Attach a click handler to the `#mapLocation` button. The function sets the window location to a standard Google Maps URL. If the Maps application is available, it will launch. Otherwise, the URL will load in a browser. The `z` value sets the initial zoom level; the string before the @ symbol will be used as the label for the pin that is dropped at the location. The latitude and longitude values must appear in the order shown here, separated by a comma.

⓬ Call the `goTo()` method of the jQTouch object to make the Inspect Entry panel slide up into view.

⓭ Define the error callback function.

Now you need to give your app permission to access location data. Locate *Android-Manifest.xml* in the Package Explorer and double-click it. Click the AndroidManifest.xml tab at the bottom of the Android Manifest page to edit its raw XML. Then, add the lines shown in bold just below the `uses-sdk`:

```
<uses-sdk android:minSdkVersion="7" />
<uses-permission android:name="android.permission.ACCESS_COARSE_LOCATION"/>
<uses-permission android:name="android.permission.ACCESS_FINE_LOCATION"/>
```

Next, choose Run→Run in Eclipse to run the app. Try adding an entry, and then tap the new entry to bring up the Inspect Entry panel. You'll see GPS coordinates, as well as an option to map the location.

Accelerometer

Next, let's set up Kilo to duplicate the last entry in the list by shaking the phone. Add the following function to the end of *kilo.js*:

```
function dupeEntryById(entryId) {
  if (entryId == undefined) {❶
    alert('You have to have at least one entry in the list to shake a dupe.');
  } else {
    db.transaction(❷
      function(transaction) {
        transaction.executeSql(
          'INSERT INTO entries (date, food, calories, latitude, longitude) ' +❸
            'SELECT date, food, calories, latitude, longitude ' +
            'FROM entries WHERE id = ?;',
          [entryId], ❹
          function() {❺
              refreshEntries();
          },
          errorHandler❻
        );
      }
    );
  }
  startWatchingShake();❼
}
```

❶ This line makes sure an `entryId` was passed to the function. If not, the user is notified.

❷ Begin the usual database transaction steps.

❸ Define an `INSERT` statement that copies the values from the specified `entryId`. This is a type of query you haven't seen before. Instead of using a list of values for the `INSERT`, this takes the values from the results of a `SELECT` query for the specified `entryId`.

❹ Pass the `entryId` into the prepared statement, replacing the ? in the `SELECT` query with the value of the `entryId`.

❺ On success, call `refreshEntries()`, which will display the newly copied entry.

❻ On error, call the standard SQL error handler.

❼ As you'll see later, we're going to avoid collecting multiple shake events by disabling the shake detection while we're in this function. This will re-enable it when we're done.

Now we need to tell the application when to start and stop watching the accelerometer. We'll set it up to start watching when the Date panel finishes sliding into view and to stop listening when the panel starts sliding out. To do this, we just need to add the following lines to the document ready function in *kilo.js*:

```
$('#date').bind('pageAnimationEnd', function(e, info){❶
    if (info.direction == 'in') {❷
        startWatchingShake();
```

```
        }
    });
    $('#date').bind('pageAnimationStart', function(e, info){❸
        if (info.direction == 'out') {❹
            stopWatchingShake();
        }
    });
```

❶ Bind an anonymous handler to the **pageAnimationEnd** event of the #date panel. Pass the event and the additional information in as parameters.

❷ Check to see if the **direction** property of the info object equals **in**. If it does, call the **startWatchingShake()** function, which we'll look at shortly.

❸ Bind an anonymous handler to the **pageAnimationStart** event of the #date panel. Pass the event and the additional information in as parameters.

❹ Check to see if the **direction** property of the info object equals **out**. If it does, call the **stopWatchingShake()** function, which we'll look at shortly.

Technically, we can bind to just one of the page animation events, like so:

```
$('#date').bind('pageAnimationEnd', function(e, info){
    if (info.direction == 'in') {
        startWatchingShake();
    } else {
        stopWatchingShake();
    }
});
```

The reason I didn't do this is that stopWatchingShake() will not be called until after the page animation is complete. Therefore, the accelerometer will be actively watched during the page transition, which can sometimes result in choppy animation.

All that's left for us to do is write the **startWatchingShake()** and **stopWatchingShake()** functions. Add the following functions to the end of *kilo.js*:

```
function startWatchingShake() {❶
    var lastReading = null;❷
    var threshold = 10;❸
    var success = function(coords){❹
        var current = coords.x + coords.y + coords.z;
        if (lastReading != null) {❺
            if (Math.abs(current - lastReading) > threshold) {❻
                var entryId = $('#date ul li:last').data('entryId');❼
                stopWatchingShake();❽
                dupeEntryById(entryId);❾
            }
        }
        lastReading = current;
    };
```

```
        var error = function(){};❿
        var options = {};⓫
        options.frequency = 250;⓬
        sessionStorage.watchId =
            navigator.accelerometer.watchAcceleration(success, error, options);⓭
    }
    function stopWatchingShake() {⓮
        navigator.accelerometer.clearWatch(sessionStorage.watchId);⓯
    }
```

❶ Begin the `startWatchingShake()` function. This function will be called when the #date panel finishes animating into view.

❷ `lastReading` will contain the last reading so we can compare it with our current reading.

❸ Define the threshold for the shake. The higher the number, the harder the user will have to shake.

❹ Begin defining the success handler. It accepts a `coordinates` object as its sole parameter.

❺ The first time through, `lastReading` will be undefined, so we don't want to check it just yet.

❻ Check to see if the sum of the coordinates have exceeded the threshold.

❼ Get the `entryId` of the last entry on the #date panel.

❽ Disable shake detection for now (we'll re-enable it at the end of the `dupeEntryById` function).

❾ Call the `dupeEntryById()` function.

❿ Define an empty error handler.

⓫ Define an options object to pass in to the `watchAcceleration()` method of the `accelerometer` object.

⓬ Set the `frequency` property of the options object to the number of milliseconds delay between receiving data from the accelerometer.

⓭ Call the `watchAcceleration()` method of the `accelerometer` object, passing in the success handler, the error handler, and the options object as parameters. Store the result in `sessionStorage.watchId`, which we'll need for the `stopWatchingShake()` function.

⓮ Begin the `stopWatchingShake()` function. This function will be called when the #date panel starts animating out of view.

⓯ Call the `clearWatch()` method of the `accelerometer` object, passing it the `watchId` from session storage.

What You've Learned

In this chapter, you've learned how to load your web app into PhoneGap, how to install your app on your phone, and how to access five device features that are unavailable to browser-based web apps (beep, alert, vibrate, geolocation, and accelerometer).

In the next chapter, you'll learn how to package your app as an executable and submit it to the Android Market.

CHAPTER 8

Submitting Your App to the Android Market

Finally, the moment you've been waiting for: submitting your completed app to the Android Market. The process is actually pretty straightforward: you just need to prepare a release version of the app and upload it.

Preparing a Release Version of Your App

You need to do a few things to get the app ready for distribution:

- Remove any debugging or logging code
- Version the app
- Compile the app
- Sign the compiled app with a private key

Removing Debug Code

There's no reason to have debugging or logging code slowing down your app while it's running on a user's phone. If you have added any such code (see "The JavaScript Console" on page 119) to your HTML, CSS, or JavaScript files, now's the time to take it out.

You should also open up the *AndroidManifest.xml* file: in Eclipse, locate *Android Manifest.xml* in the Package Explorer and double-click it. Next, click the Android-Manifest.xml tab at the bottom of the Android Manifest page to edit its raw XML. Then, search for "debuggable" and set it to false. When you're done, it should look something like this:

```
...
<application
    android:icon="@drawable/ic_launcher"
    android:label="@string/app_name"
    android:debuggable="false">
...
```

While you have the manifest file open, you might as well ensure that `android:icon` and `android:label` are specified as shown in the previous listing. You're probably using the default icon that's used by Android. You should prepare an icon for your app in several resolutions and place them in the appropriate subdirectory in the Package Explorer:

res/drawable-hdpi/ic_launcher.png
    72 × 72 pixels

res/drawable-ldpi/ic_launcher.png
    36 × 36 pixels

res/drawable-mdpi/ic_launcher.png
    48 × 48 pixels

Google has published a set of icon design guidelines, including an icon template pack you can download. See *http://developer.android.com/guide/practices/ui_guidelines/icon _design.html*.

Versioning Your App

Near the top of your *AndroidManifest.xml* file, you should see values set for the version name and version code for your app:

```
...
<manifest
    xmlns:android="http://schemas.android.com/apk/res/android"
    package="com.jonathanstark.kilo"
    android:versionCode="1"
    android:versionName="1.0">
...
```

Because this is probably the first version of your app, these values are fine as is. Once you've published your app and later want to release an update, you'll update these values appropriately. The Android system doesn't check or enforce this version information, but it's a critical piece of data for your long term app strategy.

The version name is the value that will be shown to the user. It's a string, so you can put whatever you want here, but the common practice is to use a `<major>.<minor>.<point>` format (such as 1.0.0).

The version code is expected to be a positive integer value. It need not correspond to the version name in any way. In fact, it probably won't—you should just increment it by 1 every time you release an update, regardless of whether the release is a major upgrade or a minor bug fix.

Compile and Sign Your App

Android requires that all apps be digitally signed by the developer. The process for doing so is easy: select your project in the Package Explorer (click *KiloForAndroid* at the top of the Package Explorer list) and then click File→Export. Open the Android folder, and choose Export Android Application. You'll be led through the following steps:

1. Select the project to export. This will default to *KiloForAndroid*. Click Next.

2. Select the key store to store your keys in. If this is your first time through, choose Create a New Keystore. Choose a secure location on your computer for the keystore, and give it a name. This keystore will contain all your private keys, so keep it safe. Use a strong password , and click Next.

3. Now you need to create a key. Fill in the fields requested (it's OK to leave some of the bottom fields blank if you don't have applicable values), including a password for the private key portion of this key, and the number of years it should be valid for. Click Next.

4. Choose where to save the compiled and signed Android package (APK) file. Give it the name *KiloForAndroid.apk*.

When you're done, you'll have a signed app (*KiloForAndroid.apk*) in the destination you selected. Next time you export it, you need to only supply the password for your keystore and the key you wish to sign the app with.

 Do not lose either your keystore or key password. If you forget either password or lose the keystore or key file, you won't be able to update your app once it's published.

Uploading Your App to the Android Market

All that is left to do is upload the signed binary to the Android Market.

 You need to be a registered Android Developer to upload your app. If have not already registered, you can do so at *http://market.android.com/ publish/signup*. The process is quick and easy—you just fill out a bit of profile information (name, email, phone, etc.), pay a $25 registration fee (using Google Checkout), and agree to the Android Market Developer Distribution Agreement.

1. Launch your web browser, navigate to *http://market.android.com/publish/*, and sign into your Google account.

2. If you aren't forwarded automatically after logging in, navigate to *http://market .android.com/publish/Home* and click the Upload Application button (Figure 8-1).

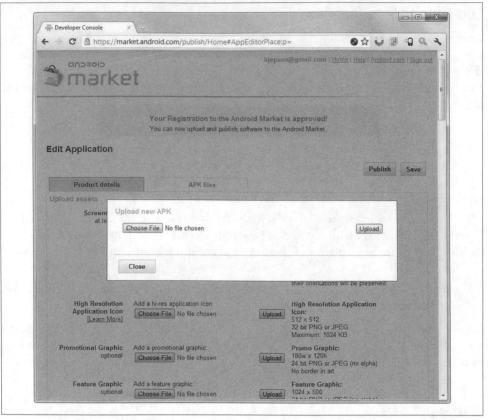

Figure 8-1. Navigate to the Android Market upload page to submit your app

3. Click the Choose File button under "Upload New APK," browse to *KiloFor Android.apk* on your hard drive, and click the Upload button. You'll be notified about the permissions that your app requires (users will be warned about these permissions when they go to install your app). Click Save to save the app you just uploaded.

4. You can upload a couple of screenshots to be displayed on the Market page for your app. You need at least two. To take a screenshot of your app, launch your app from within Eclipse, choose Window→Open Perspective→Other, and choose DDMS. Select your device from the Devices list, and click the Screen Capture icon (it looks like a small camera).

5. Upload a high resolution icon for your app. You can also provide Promotional graphics and video.

6. Enter a title for your app in the Listing Details section (30 characters max).

7. Enter a description for your app (4000 characters max), along with a list of recent changes to the app and some promotional text.

8. Select a type and category for your app.

9. Specify a price for your app.

10. Indicate your copy protection, content rating and location preferences in the Publishing Options section.

11. Enter your website address, email address, and phone number in the Contact Information section.

12. Agree to the terms in the Consent section.

13. Click the Publish button.

Congrats! Your app will be available in the Android Market almost immediately.

Distributing Your App Directly

One very attractive feature of the Android platform is that it lets developers skip the Android Market completely and distribute apps directly to users. This is a great option in many situations. For example, a corporate IT department might want to distribute a private app to employees. Or maybe you want to run a private beta of your app before uploading it to the Android Market.

Whatever the case, direct distribution couldn't be easier: upload your signed *.apk* binary to your web server and provide your users with a link to it. Users click the link—say, from an email message or a web page—and the app is downloaded and installed. Simple.

> You can also use QR codes to distribute links to your app. A QR code is a two-dimensional barcode that can store up to 4,296 alphanumeric characters of arbitrary text and be read by the camera on an Android phone. When a user encounters your QR code, she can take a picture of it with Google Goggles (or another QR code reader app), and she'll be provided with a link to your app. You can learn more by visiting the Google Chart Tools page devoted to QR codes (*http://code.google.com/apis/chart/docs/gallery/qr_codes.html*). You can create your own for free using Google's Live Chart Playground (*http://code.google.com/apis/chart/docs/chart_playground.html*).

The only caveat is that users have to first allow installation of non-Market applications by navigating to Settings→Applications and enabling the Unknown Sources option (Figure 8-2). If the user has not first enabled downloads from unknown sources, he will still be allowed to download the app, but will be alerted that the install is blocked (Figure 8-3). The alert dialog will allow him to navigate directly to the relevant setting or cancel the installation. When the user first activates the checkbox, he'll see a confirmation dialog that warns him about the implications of his choice (Figure 8-4).

Figure 8-2. Users can opt to download applications from sources other than the Android Market

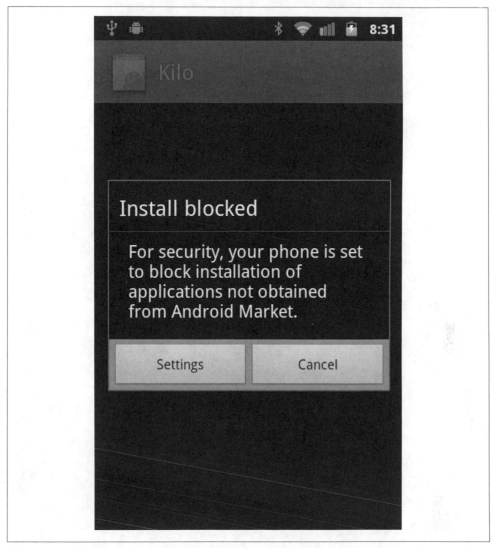

Figure 8-3. If the user attempts to install an app from an unknown source without having checked the appropriate setting, he will be prompted to change the setting or cancel the installation process

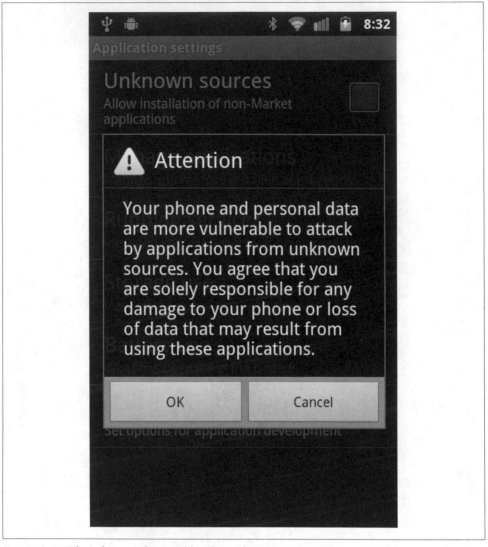

Figure 8-4. When the user first enables the Unknown Sources option, he'll be presented with a confirmation dialog that warns him about the implications

Further Reading

If you'd like to dig deeper into the mechanics of the Android SDK, the best place to start is the excellent online documentation available at *http://developer.android.com/*. Here are some other resources that I find useful and refer to often:

- Android Discuss mailing list (*http://groups.google.com/group/android-discuss*)
- Android Developers mailing list (*http://groups.google.com/group/android-developers*)
- jQTouch mailing list (*http://groups.google.com/group/jqtouch*)
- PhoneGap mailing list (*http://groups.google.com/group/phonegap*)
- Android reference for WebView (*http://developer.android.com/reference/android/webkit/WebView.html*)
- Android reference for WebChromeClient (*http://developer.android.com/reference/android/webkit/WebChromeClient.html*)
- Android reference for WebViewClient (*http://developer.android.com/reference/android/webkit/WebViewClient.html*)
- Android reference for WebSettings (*http://developer.android.com/reference/android/webkit/WebSettings.html*)

 The Android references in the list above are interesting only if you want to start digging around in the PhoneGap source code or maybe write your own native HTML app wrapper. WebView is the primary class and it's used to display HTML; by default, it doesn't support JavaScript, browser widgets (e.g., location bar, back/forward buttons), or error handling.

The other three classes extend the WebView in various ways. WebChromeClient adds support for JavaScript dialogs, favicons, titles, and progress indicators. WebViewClient adds support for some useful event listeners like `onFormResubmission()`, `onPageStarted()`, and `onPageFinished()`. Finally, WebSettings gives you access to the WebView settings state with methods such as `getDatabaseEnabled()` and `setUserAgentString()`.

Again, you won't need to worry about these unless you want to get into the Java code under the hood.

Now get out there and make some great Android apps!

Detecting Browsers with WURFL

WURFL (Wireless Universal Resource File) is an XML file that contains the information needed to identify a wide range of mobile devices. On its own, it doesn't do anything. But if you use one of the many available libraries for it, you can create web apps that can figure out what kind of device has connected to your app.

For example, wurfl-php (*http://wurfl.sourceforge.net/nphp/*) lets you detect which operating system a remote device is running from within a PHP script.

 To use WURFL and wurfl-php, you'll need to be running your web app on a hosting provider that supports PHP. You'll also need to understand how to install files and PHP libraries onto your server. In this appendix, I show you how to do this using the Unix or Mac OS X command line. If you are uncomfortable with any of this, but are comfortable working with PHP, contact your hosting provider's support department and ask if they'd be willing to install WURFL and wurfl-php on the server you use. If you're using a shared server, it would give your hosting provider a competitive advantage to offer this feature to all their customers.

Installation

First, download wurfl-php and extract it somewhere on your server (in general, it's best to not put libraries in your public web folder, so I'm putting it into the *src* directory in my home directory). Replace *~/src* with the location you want to install it to and replace *wurfl-php-1.3.1.tar.gz* with the name of the file you actually downloaded:

```
$ mkdir ~/src
$ cd ~/src
$ tar xvfz ~/Downloads/wurfl-php-1.3.1.tar.gz
```

Next, download the latest WURFL file (*http://sourceforge.net/projects/wurfl/files/WURFL/*), copy it into the wurfl-php folder, and gunzip it (see the wurfl-php documentation for tips on using this file in its compressed state). Replace *~/src/wurfl-php-1.3.1/* with the full path to the directory that was created in the previous step when you extracted the wurfl-php distribution, and replace *~/Downloads/wurfl-latest.xml.gz* with the path to the WURFL distribution that you downloaded:

```
$ cd ~/src/wurfl-php-1.3.1/
$ cp ~/Downloads/wurfl-latest.xml.gz .
$ gunzip wurfl-latest.xml.gz
```

Finally, download the desktop web browser patch so WURFL doesn't encounter errors when someone visits your page from a desktop browser:

```
$ curl -O http://wurfl.sourceforge.net/web_browsers_patch.xml
```

Configuration

Create the following wurfl-config file (*wurfl-config.xml*) in *~/src/wurfl-php-1.3.1/* (or the directory you created when you extracted wurfl-php):

```
<?xml version="1.0" encoding="UTF-8"?>
<wurfl-config>
  <wurfl>
    <main-file>wurfl-latest.xml</main-file>
      <patches>
        <patch>web_browsers_patch.xml</patch>
      </patches>
  </wurfl>
  <persistence>
    <provider>file</provider>
      <params>dir=./work/cache</params>
  </persistence>
</wurfl-config>
```

Create the cache directory and make sure it and its parent is writable by whichever user runs PHP scripts. If your web server is configured to run your PHP scripts under your user credentials, this step should not be necessary. As with previous examples, replace *~/src/wurfl-php-1.3.1/* with the location you created earlier. Replace *_www* with the username that your PHP scripts run under (you will need superuser credentials to run this command):

```
$ mkdir -p ~/src/wurfl-php-1.3.1/work/cache
$ sudo chown -R _www ~/src/wurfl-php-1.3.1/work
```

If any of the parent directories above your cache directory are not readable by the username that the PHP scripts run under, you won't be able to write to the cache. If WURFL reports an error writing to the cache folder, you can choose another location for it (such as */var/wurfl/cache*) and change your *wurfl-config.xml* to point to it. Before you do that, create the cache directory and give write access for it and its parent to the username that your PHP scripts run under:

```
$ sudo mkdir -p /var/www/wurfl/cache
$ sudo chown -R _www /var/www/wurfl
```

Then you'd change the persistence section of *wurfl-config.xml* as shown:

```
<persistence>
  <provider>file</provider>
    <params>dir=/var/www/wurfl/cache</params>
</persistence>
```

 If in doubt, contact your hosting provider's tech support and explain that you want the cache directory to be writable by your PHP scripts.

Testing wurfl-php

Now, in your web directory (such as *Sites* or *public_html*), create the following PHP file (name it something like *wurfl-test.php*). The first time you visit it from your Android device (or any other browser), it will take a long time as it builds the initial cache. After that, it should be zippy. Figure A-1 shows how this should appear in your browser. You can now modify this PHP code to suit your needs:

```
<html>
<head>
    <meta name="viewport" content="user-scalable=no, width=device-width" />
    <title>WURFL Test</title>
<?php

  define("WURFL_DIR", "/Users/NAME/src/wurfl-php-1.3.1/WURFL/");
  define("RESOURCES_DIR", "/Users/NAME/src/wurfl-php-1.3.1/");

  require_once WURFL_DIR . 'Application.php';

  $wurflConfigFile = RESOURCES_DIR . 'wurfl-config.xml';
  $wurflConfig = new WURFL_Configuration_XmlConfig($wurflConfigFile);
  $wurflManagerFactory = new WURFL_WURFLManagerFactory($wurflConfig);

  $wurflManager = $wurflManagerFactory->create();
  $wurflInfo = $wurflManager->getWURFLInfo();

  $requestingDevice = $wurflManager->getDeviceForHttpRequest($_SERVER);
  $is_android = FALSE;
  if ($requestingDevice->getCapability("device_os") == "Android") {
      $is_android = TRUE;
  }
?>
</head>
<body>
  <?php
    if ($is_android) {
      echo "I spy an Android phone.";
    }
```

```
?>
<ul>
  <?php
    foreach ($requestingDevice->getAllCapabilities() as $kcy => $value) {
      echo "<li>$key = $value";
    }
  ?>
</ul>
</body>
</html>
```

 I couldn't use ~, so I had to put in the full path to the WURFL stuff; replace */Users/NAME/src/wurfl-php-1.3.1/* with the full path to the *wurfl-php* directory you created earlier.

Figure A-1. Output of the sample wurfl-php script

About the Authors

Jonathan Stark is a mobile and web application consultant who has been called "an expert on publishing desktop data to the web" by the Wall Street Journal. He has written two books on web application programming, is a tech editor for both php|architect and Advisor magazines, and has been quoted in the media on Internet and mobile lifestyle trends. Jonathan began his programming career more than 20 years ago on a Tandy TRS-80 and still thinks Zork was a sweet game.

Brian Jepson is an O'Reilly editor, hacker, and co-organizer of Providence Geeks and the Rhode Island Mini Maker Faire. He's also been involved in various ways over the years with AS220, a non-profit unjuried and uncensored arts center in Providence, Rhode Island.

Colophon

The animal on the cover of *Building Android Apps with HTML, CSS, and JavaScript* is a maleo (*Macrocephalon maleo*), an endangered bird with a current population between 5,000 and 10,000 that is only found on the Indonesian islands of Sulawesi and Buton. This distinctive, rare bird is about the size of a full-grown chicken, with white and light pink belly and breast feathers standing out against its black back and wings. The maleo's scientific name indicates that individuals possess strong legs and large heads. Their sloped foreheads are often described as "helmet-shaped."

Perhaps the most remarkable characteristic of this monogamous bird is the way it nests and cares for its offspring. Unlike most birds, who incubate their own eggs, the maleo lays its eggs in pits in the sand to be incubated by the sun, geothermal energy, or both. Maleos nest communally, which is likely a defensive measure against egg predators. When a young maleo hatches and emerges from the sand after two to three months of incubation, it is independent and able to fly. It quickly heads to the forest on its own to hide from predators and find food.

Maleo eggs are approximately five times the size of a chicken egg, making them desirable among locals. In 2009, the US-based Wildlife Conservation Society purchased a 36-acre area of the Sulawesi beach (containing about 40 nests) in order to raise awareness about the steadily declining species and to protect the birds from human egg harvesters.

The cover image is from Cassell's *Natural History*. The cover font is Adobe ITC Garamond. The text font is Linotype Birka; the heading font is Adobe Myriad Condensed; and the code font is LucasFont's TheSansMonoCondensed.

Get even more for your money.

Join the O'Reilly Community, and register the O'Reilly books you own. It's free, and you'll get:

- $4.99 ebook upgrade offer
- 40% upgrade offer on O'Reilly print books
- Membership discounts on books and events
- Free lifetime updates to ebooks and videos
- Multiple ebook formats, DRM FREE
- Participation in the O'Reilly community
- Newsletters
- Account management
- 100% Satisfaction Guarantee

Signing up is easy:

1. Go to: oreilly.com/go/register
2. Create an O'Reilly login.
3. Provide your address.
4. Register your books.

Note: English-language books only

To order books online:
oreilly.com/store

For questions about products or an order:
orders@oreilly.com

To sign up to get topic-specific email announcements and/or news about upcoming books, conferences, special offers, and new technologies:
elists@oreilly.com

For technical questions about book content:
booktech@oreilly.com

To submit new book proposals to our editors:
proposals@oreilly.com

O'Reilly books are available in multiple DRM-free ebook formats. For more information:
oreilly.com/ebooks

O'REILLY®

Spreading the knowledge of innovators   oreilly.com

The information you need, when and where you need it.

With Safari Books Online, you can:

Access the contents of thousands of technology and business books

- Quickly search over 7000 books and certification guides
- Download whole books or chapters in PDF format, at no extra cost, to print or read on the go
- Copy and paste code
- Save up to 35% on O'Reilly print books
- **New!** Access mobile-friendly books directly from cell phones and mobile devices

Stay up-to-date on emerging topics before the books are published

- Get on-demand access to evolving manuscripts.
- Interact directly with authors of upcoming books

Explore thousands of hours of video on technology and design topics

- Learn from expert video tutorials
- Watch and replay recorded conference sessions

Spreading the knowledge of innovators

safari.oreilly.com